Diagonal (or On-Point) Set

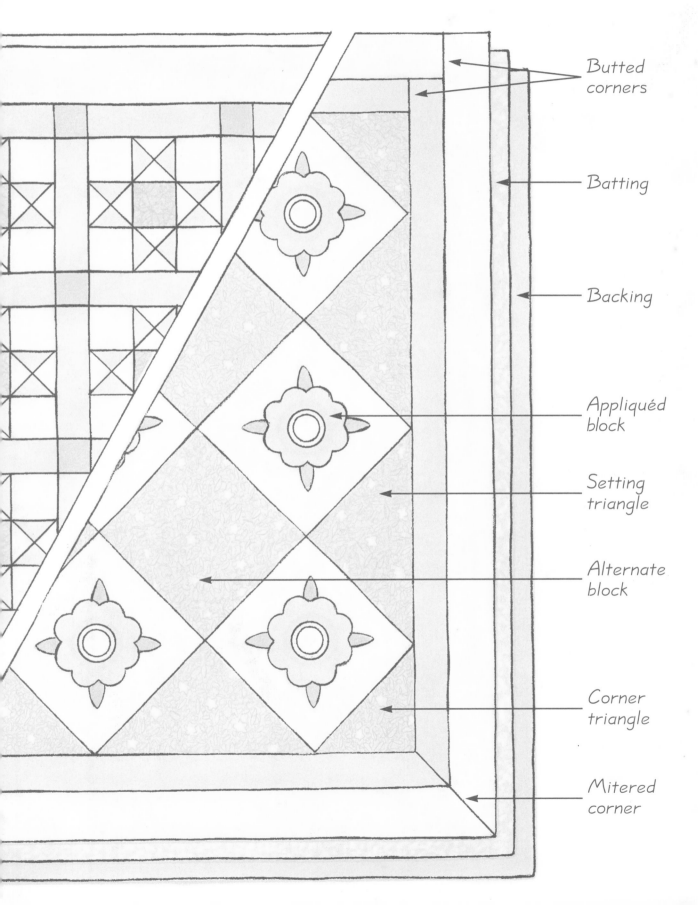

Butted corners

Batting

Backing

Appliquéd block

Setting triangle

Alternate block

Corner triangle

Mitered corner

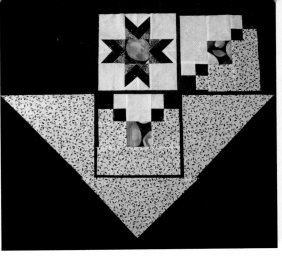

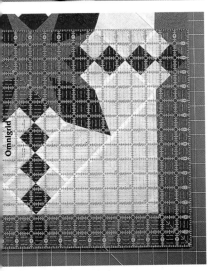

Rodale's Successful
Quilting Library™

Sensational
Sets &
Borders

Sally Schneider
Editor

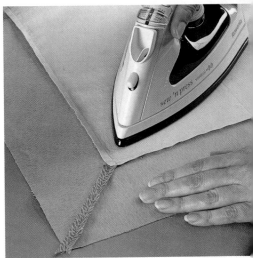

Rodale Press, Inc.
Emmaus, Pennsylvania

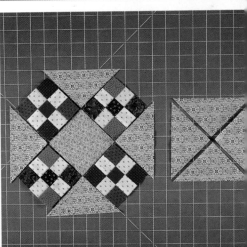

Editor: Sally Schneider
Contributing Editor: Karen Costello Soltys
Writers: Sharyn Squier Craig, Jane Hall, Dixie Haywood, Sally Schneider, Janet Wickell, Darra Duffy Williamson
Series Designer: Sue Gettlin
Design Coordinator and Cover Designer: Christopher Rhoads
Layout Designer: Keith Biery
Illustrator: Sandy Freeman
Photographers: John Hamel, Mitch Mandel
Photo Stylist: Stan Green
Photography Editor: James A. Gallucci
Model: Anne Cassar
Copy Editor: Erana C. Bumbardatore
Manufacturing Coordinator: Patrick T. Smith
Indexer: Nanette Bendyna
Editorial Assistance: Jodi Guiducci, Susan L. Nickol

On the cover and these pages: Basket of Posies by Jill Stolpestad, Batavia, Illinois

Rodale Home and Garden Books
Vice President and Editorial Director: Margaret J. Lydic
Managing Editor, Quilt Books: Suzanne Nelson
Director of Design and Production: Michael Ward
Associate Art Director: Carol Angstadt
Production Manager: Robert V. Anderson, Jr.
Studio Manager: Leslie M. Keefe
Copy Director: Dolores Plikaitis
Book Manufacturing Director: Helen Clogston
Office Manager: Karen Earl-Braymer

We're always happy to hear from you.

For questions or comments concerning the editorial content of this book, please write to:

Rodale Press, Inc.
Book Readers' Service
33 East Minor Street
Emmaus, PA 18098

Look for other Rodale books wherever books are sold. Or call us at (800) 848–4735.

For more information about Rodale Press and the books and magazines we publish, visit our World Wide Web site: http://www.rodalepress.com

Library of Congress Cataloging-in-Publication Data published the first volume of this series as:

Rodale's successful quilting library.
    p. cm.
Includes index.
    ISBN 0–87596–760–4 (hc: v. 1:alk paper)
    1. Quilting. 2. Patchwork. I. Soltys, Karen Costello. II. Rodale Press.
TT835.R622 1997
746.46'041—dc21   96–51316

Sensational Sets & Borders:
ISBN 0–87596–762–0

Distributed in the book trade by St. Martin's Press

2 4 6 8 10 9 7 5 3 1   hardcover

Contents

Introduction

Quilters everywhere seem to want to know more about sets and borders. This isn't just a hunch—we know this because we asked! When the Rodale quilt editors surveyed quilters to find the topics they wanted to learn about, this duo was at the top of the list. Figuring out the most pleasing way to arrange the blocks together and then deciding what sort of border to use to finish the whole arrangement are not matters to take lightly. These two decisions affect how successful your finished quilt will be. But we noticed that there are very few books that help quilters explore all the creative setting and border possibilities, how to choose the best one for a particular quilt, and then how to actually sit down at the sewing machine and make it all happen. There's a big gap in setting and border information, and we decided to fill it!

Working as the editor on this book was doubly exciting because I love working with borders, plus I've always wanted to explore setting options that go beyond the ordinary. I've been a quiltmaker for more than 25 years now, and I've added a lot of borders to quilts. When I first started quilting, I figured that all you had to do was cut a strip of fabric, sew it to the edge of the quilt, and trim off what was left over. As a result, many of my early quilts have very wavy borders, and no, the fullness often didn't quilt out. But once I learned the very simple basics of fitting borders to quilts, my finished pieces became much flatter, making them easier to baste, quilt, and bind.

I've been in a bit of a rut when it comes to settings, limiting myself to straight, sashed, and diagonally set quilts. As I wander through quilt shows, I find the same thing—lots of straight sets and sashing strips, some diagonal sets, and a few medallions. But I don't think I've ever seen a zigzag set, and only recently have people started putting different-size blocks together into puzzle sets.

I also know, through very reliable sources, that there are many quilters who have large stashes of blocks that they keep in boxes because they don't know how to put them all together into a quilt. Or they may have their blocks put together but they've stalled out, not sure what to do for a border. If you are in this boat, have no fear! You are not alone. With the help of the inspiring photos and illustrations in this book, plus the easy-to-understand how-to information, you won't be stalled for long.

We've assembled a very talented and creative writing team whose collective experience in quilting and teaching numbers an impressive 115 years! Sharyn Squier Craig, Jane Hall, Dixie Haywood, and Darra Duffy Williamson all drew upon their very best knowledge to share lots of secrets to success with sets and borders. I stepped outside my role as editor and turned author myself, writing the section on "painless" borders, a fun and easy quiltmaking concept I developed and taught for about 7 years. Together we've provided more than 150 tips, sprinkled throughout the book. Even if you have only a few minutes at a time to spend with this book, you'll be able to glean some very useful tricks to try the next time you sit down at your sewing machine.

To give you lots of glorious color inspiration, we scoured the country looking for great quilts to illustrate the setting and bordering ideas. The results of this search show in the quilt photographs that open each section. From beginning to end, there is inspiration in every chapter. Several sample makers plus the quilt book editors at Rodale worked with me to stitch the samples that  we photographed. Because we made these samples specifically for the book, we know that the techniques we show you will absolutely, positively work.

One of the hazards of being a quilt book editor is that you want to run right home and try out a new technique or start a new quilt every night. After working on this book, I'm anxious to try a zigzag setting—I've never done one of those—or maybe I'll gather all the sample blocks I've made over the years and put them all together into a puzzle quilt. Or maybe. . . . The possibilities are endless, and I can hardly wait!

Sally Schneider

Sally Schneider
Editor

1 To help prevent threads from tangling at the beginning of a row of stitching, lower the sewing machine needle into the fabric before lowering the presser foot.

2 When sewing a large quilt top together, place a card table or an ironing board next to your sewing machine to help support the top and to avoid drag on the needle.

3 When you purchase fabric for a quilt, purchase an extra yard or two of one of the fabrics and make pillowcases to match the quilt (use an old pillowcase for a pattern). There's no law that says your pillowcases must match your sheets, and imagine how pretty the quilt will look on a bed with coordinating pillowcases.

4 Cut the borders and larger pieces from a length of fabric first, then cut the smaller pieces from the fabric that remains. If you don't, you might end up not having enough fabric to cut the larger pieces.

5 When assembling a quilt top, fill several bobbins in advance to avoid having to stop and refill them.

6 Use thread snips or small scissors for cutting threads. Because most people tend to cut at the same spot on the scissors each time, cutting thread may create a dull spot on the blades of your fabric scissors.

7 Use the same amount of quilting in the border that you do in the body of the quilt. When areas are unevenly quilted, the less-quilted parts tend to ripple and bulge.

8 You can vary the width of the borders on a bed quilt to suit the design. If a border design is intended to cover the pillows, the top border may need to be wider. However, if the blocks will cover the pillow, it may need to be narrower. You can also eliminate a top border if that works better on your bed.

9 Cut side- and corner setting triangles from a different fabric than the background to create a border effect without adding a border.

10 If you must piece strips to achieve the needed length for a border, try to match the fabric pattern to disguise the seam. On solid fabric, plan your quilting designs so they will hide the seam.

11 Traditional measurements for sashing strips and borders provide a starting place for planning, but they are not written in stone. Fabrics, patterns, and arrangements can all conspire to make the size of your sashes and borders different. Beware only of having inordinately narrow or wide sashes and borders.

12 At every step in the construction of a quilt, it is important to square up the edges, trimming away excess fabric. Blocks must be square and sized alike. Sashes and borders will wobble if they are added to edges that are not absolutely straight. Square up the quilt after each border is added to prepare for attaching the next border.

13 When adding pieced borders to a quilt, stitch with the border on top if possible, to avoid bending seam allowances the wrong way as they go under the presser foot. If there are an equal number of seams on the quilt top and border, watch each one as it comes up to the sewing needle to keep it flat.

14 When choosing the size of motifs for the repeat in a pieced border, consider using an oversize design, such as a Dogtooth triangle, to provide a large zigzag frame for your quilt.

15 When sewing on border strips that you plan to miter, place the needle precisely next to the last stitch of the adjacent border seam. By beginning the new border seam exactly where the previous seam ends, you will avoid any gaps and will produce a perfectly mitered seam.

16 Using the block background as the sashing gives the impression that the blocks are floating, creating a subtle space around the pieced blocks.

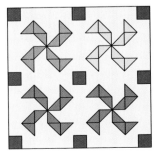

17 When you prepare diagonally set quilts for basting, remember that the lengthwise and crosswise directions are on the bias grain of the fabric. Always smooth diagonally set quilts with the straight grain of the fabric, running your hands diagonally along the top of the quilt.

18 Try coloring the block used in the main part of the quilt a different way to make it look like a pieced border. Pineapple blocks, Log Cabin blocks, and some Star blocks are particularly successful when treated this way.

19 If you're not sure what blocks set side by side will look like as a quilt, look at one or two of them through a multiview lens. This handy tool multiplies a block 25 times, so you can really see what that side-by-side set will look like before making all the blocks. Look for it at your local quilt shop or in your favorite quilting catalog.

20 When you are trying to decide which setting to use for your blocks, arrange them on the design wall (or the floor) and take a Polaroid picture of the setting. You can try many different settings in this way, and evaluate the results by looking at the photos side by side, rather than trying to remember what each one looked like.

21 If you are making a quilt for a bed, try arranging the blocks on the bed to determine the best setting.

You can spread proposed sashing fabric or alternate block fabric on the bed first to get a better idea of your finished product.

22 Baste a diagonally set quilt to the batting and backing as soon as it is completed. Because the length and width of the quilt are on the bias grain, they stretch out of shape more easily if hung on a hanger or left on a design wall for any length of time. Once the quilt top is stretched, it's almost impossible to baste it flat.

23 Instead of pins or pencils, try using a Japanese Hera marker to mark matching points for sashing strips, borders, and quilt tops. You can also use it to mark 45 degree stitching lines for mitered borders. The Hera marker isn't only for marking quilting designs!

24 Once you have decided on a setting, draw it on graph paper. You don't always have to graph the entire quilt; one-half or one-quarter of the quilt is often sufficient to check the proportions and calculate cutting dimensions.

25 Don't limit yourself to a quilt shop when looking for paper to design borders on. Try the grocery store for freezer paper, shelf paper, or waxed paper, and the art supply store for tracing paper. Your doctor's office may be able to get examining table paper for you, or check with your local newspaper for roll ends of newsprint.

Learning the
Lingo

A big part of tackling any task is understanding the language. Even the most basic arrangement of quilt blocks can include a variety of component parts, each with its own name. This chapter identifies and demystifies terms such as basic and alternate blocks, secondary pattern, sashing, cornerstones, and mixed-technique borders. Read on to brush up on all the basic elements of quilt sets and borders.

Getting Ready

Before you begin to design a set for your quilt, you will need to select the block or blocks you will use. You may already have these in mind; if not, a comprehensive book of block patterns can prove extremely helpful. Copy prospective blocks onto graph paper and color them with colored pencils to test various color schemes.

For quilters who have entered the computer world, a computer makes an excellent resource for researching block possibilities. Look for a program that includes an extensive block library or one that offers the capability to design, draw, and color your own blocks.

When you begin to construct your blocks, you'll need to have the appropriate tools on hand. In addition to basic sewing notions, you'll appreciate a rotary cutter, cutting mat, and a variety of rotary-cutting rulers.

What You'll Need

Book of quilt block designs

¼" or ⅛" graph paper and pencil

Colored pencils

Ruler

Computer and quilt design or basic drawing program (optional)

Basic Sets and Borders Vocabulary

The *set* refers to the way individual quilt blocks are arranged to form the overall design of a quilt top. A typical set might include a group of quilt blocks, with or without alternate (or secondary) blocks in between. These blocks can be placed in any number of straight or diagonal arrangements. The set might also include a variety of framing elements, either around the individual blocks or around the entire quilt.

1

2

The *basic block* is the starting point for your quilt. Usually, it is a single design that repeats in a planned pattern over the entire quilt top. An obvious exception is the sampler quilt, where each block is different.

A basic block may be entirely pieced, such as Churn Dash or Ohio Star. Or it may be all appliqué, such as a Rose in a Wreath or Baltimore Album design. Occasionally, a basic block combines piecing and appliqué. Dresden Plate and Honey Bee are good examples of this *mixed technique block.*

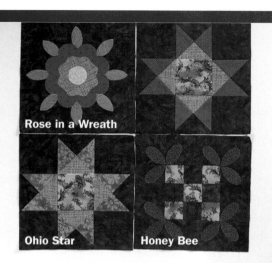

3

The introduction of an *alternate block* can dramatically alter the look of your quilt. **An alternate block separates the basic blocks in a quilt top. It can be either plain or pieced.**

Plain blocks are cut whole from a single fabric, either solid or print. You might consider selecting a variety of similarly colored fabrics, either solids or prints, rather than using a single fabric for the alternate blocks.

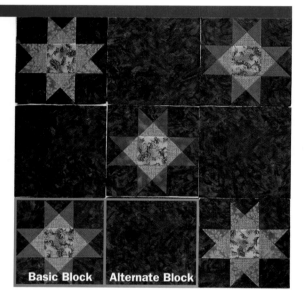

4

A *secondary pattern* occurs when the elements of a basic and an alternate block complement each other in such a way that a new, overall pattern emerges. The characteristics of the individual blocks become less obvious, while this new, overall pattern takes center stage. The resulting design can make a stunning visual statement if the two blocks are carefully chosen. Blocks based on the same grid (for example, two 9- or two 16-patch blocks) have seams that meet neatly, making them good mates for an alternate block set.

Tip

An obvious diagonal line in one block adds lots of impact when two pieced blocks are combined. The resulting secondary patterns can be especially dramatic!

***Sashing strips* are narrow strips of fabric that run vertically and horizontally between the blocks, framing each block and forming a delightful latticelike effect.** Sashing may be plain, pieced, or appliquéd. Plain sashing is cut from a solid or print fabric and involves no additional piecing or appliqué.

Pieced sashing is a combination of smaller shapes or units arranged to form a geometric design. Strips of Flying Geese units, for example, make wonderful pieced sashes. Appliqué may be stitched over plain sashing for a charming alternative treatment.

Tip

The term lattice, meaning strips between blocks, is often interchangeably with sashing.

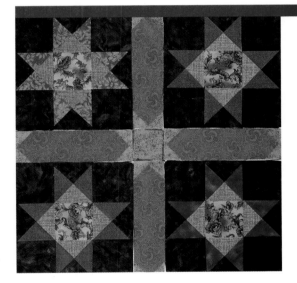

Sometimes separately cut "junction" squares, called *cornerstones,* are inserted at the corners of each block in a sashed quilt set. Cornerstones introduce a contrasting color or fabric to long sashing strips. They also allow for easier assembly and more economical use of fabric by eliminating the need for full-length sashing strips.

Best of all, cornerstones can form wonderful secondary designs, especially when combined with pieced sashing. **Try adding pieced triangles to the ends of sashing strips; a star appears as if by magic where the strips meet.**

If you consider how a painting is enhanced by a complementary frame, you will more easily understand what a carefully designed and well-proportioned *border treatment* can add to your quilt.

Most quilts are completed by framing the entire inner design area with either plain, pieced, or appliquéd strips called borders. It is not uncommon for a quilt to have more than one border, often combining two or more of these styles.

LEARNING THE LINGO

Exploring Different *Setting Options*

BLACKFORD'S BEAUTY
12 inch blocks with 4x12 inch sash...
plus 4x4 inch 9-patch corner s...

BLACKFORD'S BEAUTY
12 inch block

...AUTY
...setting

Your basic blocks are complete, but making the blocks is only half the fun. Next comes the excitement and challenge of placing those blocks in a pleasing and balanced arrangement. Should you place them uniformly side by side, or should you playfully turn them on their ears? Should you add sashing and borders?

Consider this step a wonderful opportunity for creative play. Begin with simple straight and diagonal options. These form the nucleus for all possible sets. But don't stop there. You'll discover there's a whole world of exciting setting options to explore.

Getting Ready

If you prefer seeing the entire quilt planned before you cut the first patch, you will probably enjoy designing on graph paper. To save time, make multiple copies of the block on a photocopier, then cut out and rearrange them. Or, if you have access to a computer, try a good quilt design or drawing program.

Coloring and preplanning too tedious? Make the blocks and audition the various setting possibilities on a design wall. This is a wall, a large piece of cardboard, or a sheet of foam-center insulation board covered with felt or flannel. The blocks stick to the wall without pins. You can arrange blocks on the wall and stand back to see the effect, then easily rearrange them to try another idea.

▶ *See the directions for making a design wall on page 19.*

See the directions for making a design wall on page 19.

What You'll Need

- **¼" or ⅛" graph paper and pencil**
- **Colored pencils**
- **Ruler**
- **Photocopy machine (optional)**
- **Paper scissors**
- **Glue stick**
- **Computer and quilt design or basic drawing program (optional)**
- **Design wall (see page 19)**

Setting Options

Side-by-Side Set

Fox and Geese block

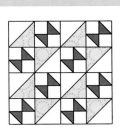

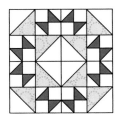

Orientation describes the way you point the blocks in your quilt. The simplest orientation is to place blocks head on—or straight—with the sides of each block parallel to the quilt's side edges. **Basic blocks, repeated side by side in vertical and horizontal rows, form the straight *side-by-side set*.**

There can be a sweet simplicity in this straightforward arrangement, especially if you favor a traditional look. However, when the side-by-side blocks, such as the Fox and Geese blocks shown, form a powerful secondary pattern, the look can be quite contemporary.

Alternating Block Set

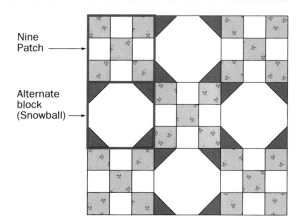

Nine Patch

Alternate block (Snowball)

An *alternate block,* either plain or pieced, inserted between each pieced basic block, brings a new dimension to the side-by-side set. It provides a visual "resting spot" between busy main blocks, and it can be a lifesaver when basic blocks are not quite the same size (no seams to match when joining blocks!). It can also provide a showcase for a special quilting pattern.

A carefully selected, pieced alternate block can create a dynamite secondary pattern. Experiment first on paper to be certain you have made a good match between the basic and alternate blocks.

Sashed Set

Add a twist to the side-by-side set with the addition of *sashing* and *cornerstones* between the basic blocks. Sashing can provide a visual break for an overpowering side-by-side set or allow for a bit of "fudging" when pieced blocks are not identical in size. It frames (and thus highlights) each individual block, forming an attractive overall lattice effect.

When joined to sashing strips at the intersection of each block, cornerstones can enhance your design by creating an exciting secondary pattern.

Sashing

Cornerstone

Diagonal Set

You'll be amazed by how a familiar block changes its appearance when it is rotated to stand *on point*. The new, *diagonal* direction adds movement and excitement, particularly for blocks with lots of squares, such as the traditional Nine Patch.

Consider setting your blocks in diagonal rows with corner and side-setting triangles filling in the spaces around the edges. Squares become diamonds, triangles tip, and the ultimate result is often more visually striking than the straight set.

Weather Vane

While a repeated-block side-by-side diagonal set is exciting in itself, consider other options as well. Just as in a straight set, a plain alternate block can simplify an overly active secondary pattern or ease the task of joining unevenly sized pieced blocks. **On the other hand, a well-chosen pieced alternate block can add extra spice to an already dynamic diagonal set.**

Tip

To stretch a limited number of blocks, add a plain alternate block to a side-by-side straight or diagonal set, and instantly double your block count!

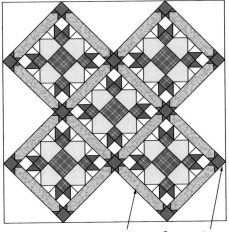

Pieced sashing   Cornerstone

Adding sashing, with or without cornerstones, to a diagonal set offers all the advantages of its sashed straight-set cousin. Plus, it still retains the added visual excitement characteristic of its on-point orientation. Pieced (rather than plain) sashing and cornerstones present even more options.

Remember that you'll need large side-setting triangles to finish the diagonal rows in every on-point set. Instructions for measuring, cutting, and incorporating these triangles are discussed in "The Basics of Diagonal Sets" on page 30.

The *bar or strippy set* is characterized by a strong linear pattern that runs either vertically or horizontally across the surface of the quilt. Blocks touch each other in one direction and are separated by sashing in the other. This creates a series of alternating pieced and plain strips.

Blocks may be set on point, straight, or in any combination of the two. They may repeat the same pattern, vary from row to row, or differ completely for a true sampler-style strippy quilt.

Tip

Striped fabric adds visual excitement to the plain rows in a strippy quilt. For another attractive alternative, try appliqué on some of the plain strips.

EXPLORING DIFFERENT SETTING OPTIONS

Zigzag Set

There is no rule dictating that quilt blocks must line up soldier-straight in every quilt. The *zigzag set* makes a wonderful alternative to the more traditional options.

Staggered rows can run either vertically or horizontally across the quilt top. **Blocks can be set straight or on point and staggered evenly; an alternate-row, half-block drop is the most common arrangement.** Or they can be staggered unevenly, with random-width sashing between the blocks and rows for a more whimsical effect.

Medallion Set

The typical *medallion* quilt features a strong central motif enhanced by a series of complementary borders. The center may be a single large block or a series of blocks set either straight or on point. It must be strong enough to focus attention and designed to move the eye toward the edges.

The surrounding borders can be any combination of plain strips, appliqué, and piecework. To unify the overall design, it is vital that borders be well-balanced and proportioned, and that they repeat some of the key colors and shapes of the central motif.

Tip

Of all the settings, the medallion set presents the greatest creative and technical challenge.

Multiple Block Medallion Set

A popular variation of the medallion set is the *multiple block medallion*. In this version, the central motif is ringed entirely with borders of complete quilt blocks (such as Ohio Star) and familiar pieced units (such as Flying Geese and Checkerboards). These blocks and units are both visually powerful and easily recognizable.

There is also much less empty space in the form of side-setting triangles and border strips than in the traditional medallion set. As a result, the central unit has a more subtle impact.

The Quilter's
Problem Solver

Designing Dilemmas

Problem	Solution
Your workroom won't accommodate a permanently installed design wall.	❑ Staple felt or flannel (batting also works) over stretcher bars, like an artist's canvas. ❑ Tape felt or flannel over a cardboard panel. ❑ Turn under the ends of a length of felt or flannel and stitch to make a sleeve. Insert a yardstick or dowel in each end and drape it over a doorway. To store your temporary wall, pin sheets of tissue paper (the gift box variety) over the unfinished project, then roll it up until you are ready to work again.
Cramped work-space prevents viewing your work from optimum distance.	Lengthen your visual distance by viewing your quilt: ❑ Through a "peep hole," like those found in hotel room doors. (Check your local hardware or building supply store.) ❑ Through a reducing glass, camera, or the wrong end of binoculars. Each reduces the image, making it seem farther away. Or, try a multiview lens to see how multiple blocks would look.

Skill Builder

There are many advantages to using a design wall.

❑ It improves your perspective by allowing you to see your work head-on.

❑ You can step back and view your quilt from a distance, allowing you to assess fabric interactions and set effectiveness.

❑ Rearranging blocks on a wall can result in exciting new ideas that you couldn't have dreamed up on the design wall in your head.

❑ It allows you to design as you go, free to make changes throughout the design process.

Try This!

A design wall makes a terrific addition to your sewing space.

It allows you to audition various block arrangements and setting pieces "in the cloth" before the quilt is sewn together. It can be simple or elaborate, large or small, affixed to the wall or freestanding, depending upon your circumstances and workspace.

The ideal surface is white cotton material such as felt, flannel (or a flannel-backed tablecloth), or cotton batting. The nap acts like a magnet, so you can arrange and rearrange blocks without the bother of pinning.

EXPLORING DIFFERENT SETTING OPTIONS

The ABCs of *Settings*

Fitting the various parts of a quilt top—blocks, setting squares and triangles, sashing, and cornerstones—into a neat, attractive set is a lot like assembling a giant jigsaw puzzle. With a well-planned piecing strategy, the proper tools, and good basic construction skills, you'll meet the challenge squarely! Your quilt will grow before your eyes with speed, ease, and accuracy.

Getting Ready

What You'll Need

Completed quilt blocks

Iron and ironing board

Rotary cutter and mat

12½" square or larger rotary ruler

Seam ripper

Sewing machine

Thread

Pins

Muslin

Ironing board cover with premarked grid (optional)

Design wall (optional—see page 19)

Fabric for setting pieces

Big Board (optional)

The first and most important step in setting a quilt top together is to make certain that all of the blocks are the same size. In a perfect world, all blocks will be the identical size from the outset! It soon becomes apparent, however, that no matter how carefully they are handled, slight variations in the sizes of the blocks tend to occur through the normal processes of cutting, stitching, and pressing.

Carefully press all the blocks first, then sort them into three piles: too large, too small, and just right. Steps 1 and 2 below and on page 22 will help you deal with these blocks.

Once your quilt blocks are properly sized, you can begin the exciting process of arranging and stitching them together. Read on to discover the nuts and bolts of layout, pinning, sewing, and pressing that will make the setting process a breeze.

ABCs of Settings

1

Trim oversize blocks with a rotary cutter and ruler. Select a square ruler at least as large as the desired size of the quilt block, including seam allowances. Place the oversize block right side up on your cutting mat. **Align the ruler over the block so that the excess extends beyond the ruler's edge. Use any seam lines or diagonals on the block as guides in positioning the ruler.** Measure carefully so that the block finishes to the proper size, the motif is still centered, and you are not chopping off points or eliminating seam allowances. Trim the excess with your rotary cutter.

2

For undersize blocks, undo and restitch inaccurate seams if necessary. Avoid cutting off points or causing distortion. If the blocks are still too small, try blocking them to size. Make a blocking grid by drawing a square the proper size (including seam allowances) on a piece of muslin. Pin the muslin to the ironing board top, then pin each undersize block to the muslin. **Steam press the block, stretching the edges slightly so they align with the blocking guide.**

3

Arrange the blocks on your design surface in the layout you have chosen. Add any setting pieces required. Stand back and reevaluate your set, double-checking for balance of color and design, and for overall appeal. Make any necessary adjustments.

Number the columns across the top, starting with the upper left corner. Pin a scrap of paper (or use a piece of masking tape) with the appropriate number to the first block in each column. This will identify which column you are working on, as well as which edge of the block is the top.

4

Remove the first column from the design wall, stacking the blocks right side up in sequence. The first block (the one with the number) should be on top. Remove the second column in the same manner, then place both stacks on the table next to your sewing machine. **The stack numbered one should be on the left, and the stack numbered two should be on the right.**

5

Pick up the block on the right. Place it, right sides together, on top of the block on the left. Holding the side that is to be sewn, carefully align the edges. Pin the beginning and end of the seam line, then any key points or matching seams.

Sew the blocks together; do not cut the thread. Pick up the next block on each stack, pin, and sew. Be sure to keep the blocks in the proper order and to start sewing at the top edge of the block. Chain stitch the remaining pairs of blocks in the same manner.

6

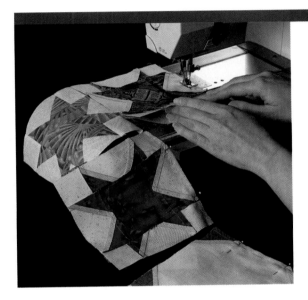

Pick up the next column of blocks and place them on the table (or on your lap) with the top edge of the blocks facing away from you. Pick up the first block in the stack. **Without cutting any threads, pin the left edge to the right edge of the first block in column two, right sides together.** Stitch them together, then add a block to the end of each row in sequence in the same manner. Continue adding all the rows of blocks in this manner.

7

When all the blocks are assembled into rows, arrange the quilt wrong side up on the ironing board. Do not clip the threads. Press the rows of blocks before joining them to form the quilt top. **Whenever possible, press opposing seams in opposite directions.** This distributes the bulk of the seam allowances evenly, resulting in smooth, accurate intersections.

Pin the rows together, matching seams and any other key points. Sew the rows together. Finish by carefully pressing the entire quilt top first from the wrong side, then from the right side.

Tip

When many points intersect or there is a lot of bulk, press the seams open to avoid lumps and distortions.

THE ABCs OF SETTINGS

The Basics
of Straight Sets

N eat, crisp, clean. In its apparent simplicity, the side-by-side set might be considered *the journeyman set of the quiltmaking world. But don't be misled! This seemingly humble arrangement of blocks offers countless opportunities for creative quilt design. The visual power of repeating side-by-side blocks, the thrill of the hunt for a compatible alternate block, and the dramatic surprise of secondary patterns lift this straightforward set to the heights of versatility.*

Getting Ready

Since a straight set is constructed entirely of straight-up, side-by-side blocks with no additional bells and whistles, it is probably the easiest of all to plan. While not particularly difficult, assembling certain variations of this familiar set can prove challenging.

When pieced and unpieced blocks alternate, the plain block acts as a seamless spacer between its pieced companions, eliminating the need to match points and seams in adjacent blocks. However, when the set is composed entirely of pieced blocks, extra care must be taken so that the points and seams of adjacent blocks meet accurately and so the quilt top finishes flat, square, and free from visual distortion. But don't worry. Coupled with the basics in "The ABCs of Settings" on page 20, this chapter provides you with the know-how to tackle either variation with skill and confidence.

Side-by-Side Sets

The side-by-side straight set is a great choice when you want a quick, uncomplicated arrangement that requires limited planning. Since it requires no additional setting pieces (sashing, cornerstones, setting squares, or setting triangles), the math involved is relatively simple.

It is a particularly good set if you use blocks that have strong diagonals, such as a diagonal row of squares or triangles. You can rotate the blocks in different directions to produce some stunning effects.

Tip

If your blocks vary in size, even by as little as ³⁄₁₆", a setting where exact sizes are not crucial might be a better choice.

2

Measure the top of the bed for which you are planning the quilt. Determine how far you want the quilt to fall on each side (drop). Add these measurements (drop on both sides) to the width of the mattress. The total will be the width of your quilt.

Add the single drop measurement to the length of the mattress to allow for the drop at the foot at the bed. If you want the quilt to go over the pillows, add another 5 to 10 inches to the length for the pillow tuck. The total measurement will be the length of your quilt.

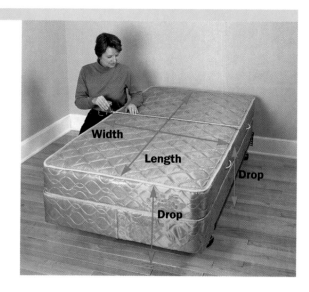

Tip

A common drop measurement is 10" to 12", but a quilt can also go all the way to the floor.

3

To determine the number of blocks required, first decide if you want borders, then assign them a proposed measurement. You can always adjust this to fit your chosen blocks and quilt size. Double the border measurement (two borders), then subtract it from both the length and width of your quilt. This is your target measurement. **Divide the target width measurement by your preferred block size, and round to the nearest whole number.** This is the number of blocks needed for each horizontal row. Repeat with the length measurement. Multiply the lengthwise blocks by the crosswise blocks for the total number of blocks required.

Tip

Try different block sizes if your calculations produce a quilt that has too few blocks in one direction, and too many in the other.

4

A plain, unpieced alternate block reinforces the formal, traditional look of straight-set blocks. With no seams to match, this set is fast and simple to piece, and it is a forgiving solution for combining off-size blocks. **Use it to stretch a limited collection of special blocks (such as friendship blocks),** focus attention on a dynamite basic block, tame a busy side-by-side set, or break up a lackluster secondary pattern.

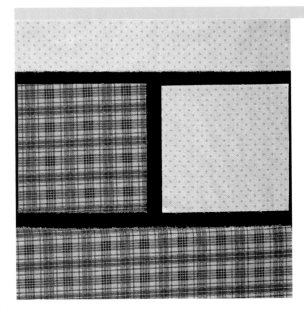

When selecting a print fabric for plain blocks, examine it carefully before cutting. Some print fabrics—including plaids, stripes, and checks—are obviously geometric. Others are more subtle, with motifs that appear random, but actually repeat in a linear fashion. If it is important to your quilt design that the fabric pattern appears straight, make sure that the fabric is printed parallel to the grain line. **When the fabric is printed off-grain like the ones shown, the squares will look like they were cut crooked.**

Audition fabrics for the alternate blocks. Select a variety of possible candidates from your fabric stash, and spread them out one or two at a time. A design wall can provide a good vantage point for viewing the selections.

Position one or two rows of basic blocks on the test fabrics, leaving spaces to represent the plain alternate blocks. Try any number of fabrics until you find the one you like best.

If you prefer to use a variety of fabrics rather than a single one for the unpieced blocks, experiment with their placement.

Tip

Use a Polaroid camera to record your favorites among the various possibilities. You can review and compare them before making your final choice.

Hourglass

Snowball

Nine Patch Variation

Pieced alternate blocks add yet another dimension to the setting riddle. Some fairly simple designs serve well in the role of alternate blocks. **Try the Snowball or Hourglass block, or this Nine Patch variation with your designs,** and see what secondary patterns appear. Or look for other block possibilities in a book of block designs.

Tip

Change the angles in the blocks for the appearance of curves while stitching straight lines. The blocks shown combine 45 and 60 degree angles.

8

Be sure to choose a compatible mate for your basic block. Blocks based on the same division of squares (such as a Nine Patch or 16-square Four Patch) generally marry well. **They are also easier to assemble, because the seam lines and prominent points of the two blocks will meet, and the results are likely to be visually pleasing.**

An exciting match is more likely if the alternating block contains a strong diagonal element. This leads the eye to smoothly link the two blocks, emphasizing the emerging secondary pattern.

Tip

You may need to be more flexible with block size and target measurement to end up with an odd number of blocks each way.

9

An alternate-block straight set appears more balanced with an odd number of blocks both lengthwise and crosswise. To calculate the number of each block required, refer to Step 3 on page 26 to plan the layout.

Start odd-numbered rows with the basic block and even-numbered rows with the alternate block (or vice versa). **Label the block in the upper left corner Block A. Label the other block Block B.** Divide the total number of blocks by two. Round up to the next whole number to determine the number of A blocks. The rest are Bs.

10

A wonderful way to combine both the side-by-side and alternate block sets is to repeat a single block in two different color or value arrangements. This appealing variation combines simplicity and spice in a single quilt! You have only one block to piece, knowing in advance that the block-to-block seams will undoubtedly be compatible. At the same time, you'll have the visual impact of two seemingly different patterns.

Experiment on paper (or with cloth) until you find a combination that pleases you.

Triangle Tricks

Problem	Solution
Block is oriented diagonally, making a side-by-side straight set unfeasible.	Straighten the block by adding corner triangles. To determine the size triangle needed, multiply the finished block size by 0.707. Round the number up to the nearest ¼ inch, then add ⅞ inch. Cut a square that size, then cut it once diagonally for two corner triangles.
Adding alternate block to one with corner triangles makes the quilt too big.	To simulate the look of alternate blocks, play with the color placement in the corner triangles. You can make it look like the Hourglass block, a traditional alternate block. Cut the triangles for two opposite corners from one fabric, and cut the triangles for the other corners from a different fabric. Cut one square of each fabric for each block.

Skill Builder

When calculating the number of blocks required to meet a target measurement, consider how the quilt will appear on the bed.

❏ Blocks can cover the entire quilt surface or they can simply cover the mattress, with borders providing the overhang.

❏ Treat the area covering the pillows as a separate design area.

❏ Rather than breaking the quilt design with a fold at the pillow, try making matching shams or pillowcases with some of the fabrics from the quilt.

Try This!

Improve your piecing accuracy!

When tackling a particularly bulky intersection, prevent shifting and stabilize the match by placing an additional pin on either side of the pin anchoring the matching seams.

To ease fullness and improve accuracy when joining pieces, blocks, or rows, stitch with the "full" side down. Your sewing machine's feeding action will gather slight fullness in the bottom layer.

THE BASICS OF STRAIGHT SETS

The Basics of
Diagonal Sets

There is no simpler way to energize a familiar block than to turn it on point in a diagonal set. A strong diagonal line can infuse even the most conservative blocks with excitement and motion. While some blocks—like the baskets shown here—are naturals for this distinctive set, others are "sleepers." Play around with your blocks and keep your eyes open for diagonal possibilities you might have overlooked.

Getting Ready

The same basic setting options that are true for straight sets also apply to blocks set diagonally. The blocks can be set side-by-side or arranged with pieced or plain alternate blocks. The rows, though, are joined diagonally, rather than horizontally or vertically.

The key measurement in determining the finished quilt size is the corner to opposite corner, or *diagonal* measurement of the block. Any number of rows will work—it isn't necessary to consider odd or even numbers of blocks or rows if you choose an alternate block set.

A quilt that is set diagonally requires side and corner triangles to complete it. The steps that follow describe rotary-cutting methods for constructing these setting triangles, but if you prefer to use templates, you will find that information in "Skill Builder" on page 35.

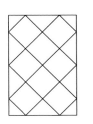

Completed quilt blocks

Calculator

¼" or ⅛" graph paper and pencil

Fabric(s) for alternate squares and setting triangles

Rotary cutter and mat

6" × 24" rotary ruler

12½" square rotary ruler

Design wall (optional)

Pins

Sewing machine

Thread

Thread snips

Iron and ironing board

THE BASICS OF DIAGONAL SETS

Diagonal Sets

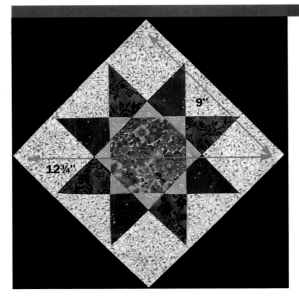

The key measurement in a diagonally set quilt is the measurement of the basic block diagonally from corner to corner, rather than along its straight side. To figure this measurement, multiply the finished size of the block by 1.414. Round the result up to the next ⅛ inch.

For example, a 9-inch block measures 12.726 inches from point to point ($9 \times 1.414 = 12.726$), rounded up to 12.75 (12¾) inches.

Tip

Since diagonal sets often involve fractional measurements, keep your calculator handy!

2

Use the diagonal measurement of the basic block to plan the overall size of the quilt. **Divide the target length of the quilt by the diagonal block size, then round it up to determine the number of blocks required lengthwise.** Repeat with the target width measurement to determine the number of blocks across the width of the quilt.

3

Arrange your blocks on a design wall or table, or sketch the layout on graph paper. Label the basic blocks (shown here as white squares). Multiply the number of blocks lengthwise by the number of blocks across to determine the total number of basic blocks.

The spaces between the basic blocks are shown here as blue squares. The blocks that go in these spaces are called the *between* or *inside* blocks. They can be pieced or plain alternate blocks, or you can fill these spaces with more basic blocks for a traditional side-by-side set. Add the between blocks to your tally.

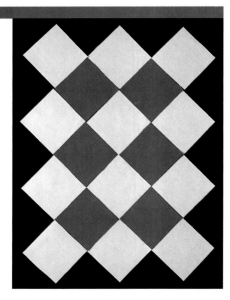

4

Tip

Cut the squares a little (½" to 1") larger. Larger triangles allow your design to "float" between the blocks and the border. You can always trim the excess.

Fill in the spaces around the edges of the quilt with triangles, called *side-setting triangles*. They are shown here as pink triangles. Cut them from large squares cut along both diagonals. (One square yields four side-setting triangles.) That way, the long (outside) edge of each triangle is on the straight grain.

Referring to your quilt diagram, count the number of side-setting triangles needed to complete your design. Divide the total by four to determine how many squares to cut. To determine the size of the square, add 1¼ inches to the diagonal measurement of the block. **Cut squares that size, then cut along both diagonals.**

Each diagonally set quilt requires four corner triangles (shown here as blue-green triangles). These should also be cut so that their outside edges are on the straight grain. **To cut these triangles, cut squares, then cut them once diagonally.** You will need two squares for each quilt.

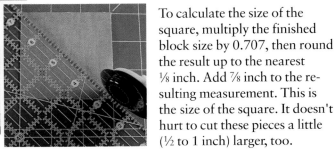

To calculate the size of the square, multiply the finished block size by 0.707, then round the result up to the nearest ⅛ inch. Add ⅞ inch to the resulting measurement. This is the size of the square. It doesn't hurt to cut these pieces a little (½ to 1 inch) larger, too.

Tip

To create a border effect without enlarging the quilt, cut setting triangles from a fabric that is different from the block background or the alternate blocks.

While it is easiest to use solid or all-over printed fabrics for the corner and side-setting triangles, you can also use directional prints and keep the lines going in the same direction. **When you cut the square for the side-setting triangles, place the top triangle on the top edge, the right-side triangle on the right side, the left-side triangle on the left side, and the bottom triangle on the bottom edge.**

Cut squares for corner triangles along opposite diagonals so that you have a triangle for each corner.

After you have pieced all the required blocks and cut all the alternate squares, side-setting triangles, and corner triangles, arrange them on your design wall or on the floor. **Start with the basic blocks, setting them on point with their corners touching.** Add any alternate blocks in the between spaces, then **arrange the side-setting and corner triangles last.**

Stand back and evaluate the arrangement, making any changes that are necessary.

THE BASICS OF DIAGONAL SETS

Tip

Check each row after it is complete to be sure all the blocks are sewn in the right direction.

8

To assemble the quilt, pick up the first two pieces (a side-setting triangle and a block) in a diagonal row. Place the side-setting triangle right sides together with the block, matching the right angle corner to the corner of the block. **Arrange the unit so that the side-setting triangle is on the bottom, then sew the two pieces together.** Place them back in the row to check that they are in the correct position, then pick up the next block (or side-setting triangle), and stitch it in place.

Sew all the blocks and side setting triangles together in diagonal rows.

9

To add the corner triangles, first fold the corner triangle in half to find the center of the long edge. Finger press a fold, or place a pin in the center.

Find the center of the side of the block to which you plan to sew the triangle, and finger press a fold or place a pin there. **Place the triangle right sides together with the block, matching the folds or pins.** Pin the pieces together at both ends and in the middle as necessary. Sew with the triangle on the bottom.

10

Press the seam allowances in each row toward the alternate blocks or the side-setting triangles. This will automatically result in butted seam allowances where blocks in different rows meet. Pin the rows together, matching seams and other important points. Sew them together. Always try to sew with the bias edge of the side-setting triangle on the bottom; this helps prevent it from stretching.

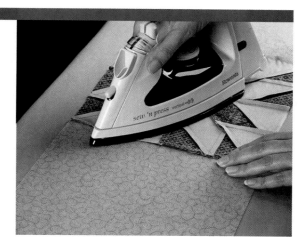

The Quilter's
Problem Solver

Dealing with Diagonals

Problem	Solution
Side-setting triangles are not straight at the outer edges.	Sewing bias seams, such as the short edges of the side-setting triangles, sometimes distorts the triangle unit. Cut the triangles oversize (add an extra inch to the size of the square), them trim the edges of the quilt top after it is assembled. Be sure to leave ¼ inch beyond the corner intersections for seam allowances. When you stitch the triangles to the blocks, align the square corner of the triangles to the corner of the blocks.
Quilt won't lie smooth for basting.	The vertical and horizontal planes of the quilt are on the bias grain, so pushing any fullness that's in the quilt toward the edges will cause lumps and bumps in the quilt top. When you smooth the quilt, pat it into place. If you must smooth it with long strokes, be sure to smooth it following the straight grain.

Skill Builder

If you prefer to make templates for the side and corner triangles, try this method.

Draw a square the finished size of the block on graph paper. Divide the square along one diagonal. This is the finished size of the side-setting triangle. Trace the triangle onto template material, adding ¼-inch seam allowances. For the corner triangle, draw a diagonal line in the other direction. Trace one of the resulting quarter-square triangles onto template material, adding the ¼-inch seam allowance. Pay particular attention to the grain line of each triangle.

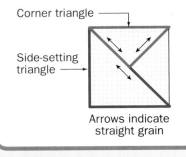

Corner triangle ⎯

Side-setting triangle ⎯

Arrows indicate straight grain

Try This!

Make half- and quarter-square versions of the basic block for the side-setting and corner triangles.

To figure the shape, size, and number of pieces necessary for these partial blocks, draft the full block on graph paper. Divide the block in half diagonally in one direction to determine the pieces required for the pieced side-setting triangle. To find the pieces required for the corner triangle, divide the block diagonally in both directions. Add appropriate seam allowance measurements to each different shape for template or rotary cutting.

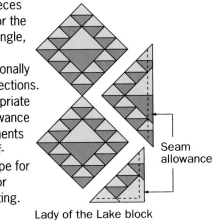

Seam allowance

Lady of the Lake block

Adding Sashing to *the Mix*

Rotary cutters to the ready! It's time to explore the magical effects that are possible when you toss humble strips and simple squares into the standard setting mix. With sashing as the catalyst, unassuming blocks take center stage, while busy blocks find room to breathe. You'll soon discover that, narrow or wide, pieced or plain, sashing strips and cornerstones add spice.

Getting Ready

As with any other set, there are times when the sashed set is the perfect choice for your quilt, and times when it is not! Sashing strips give the eye a place to rest when blocks are particularly bold or busy. They can unify diverse elements, such as sampler or scrappy blocks.

With no seams to match, sashing strips simplify the task of joining blocks not quite uniform in size. By acting as spacers, they can stretch a limited number of blocks to make a larger quilt.

From a design standpoint, sashing can create a wonderful overall lattice effect. Pairing sashing strips with cornerstones may uncover interesting secondary patterns, too. Avoid sashing, however, when your set includes plain alternate blocks (which serve the same purpose), or when side-by-side pieced blocks create appealing secondary designs.

What You'll Need

- **Completed quilt blocks**
- **Fabric for sashing and cornerstones**
- **Design wall (optional)**
- **Calculator**
- **Rotary cutter and mat**
- **6" × 24" rotary ruler**
- **¼" or ⅛" graph paper and pencil**
- **Ruler**
- **Pins**
- **Sewing machine**
- **Thread to match fabrics**
- **Thread snips**
- **Iron and ironing board**

Sashed Sets

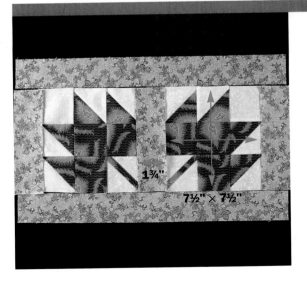

1¾"

7½" × 7½"

A good rule of thumb states that maximum sashing width should not be more than one-quarter of the finished width of the block. For example, a 12-inch block should have sashing no wider than 3 inches (plus seam allowances). Anything wider tends to overpower the block.

Minimum width is more flexible, depending on the look you want. It can range from a midwidth frame of 1 to 2 inches wide for a 12-inch block to a narrow (about ¼-inch-wide) leaded-glass effect. Just be certain that the overall result is in proportion and balanced.

2

Plain or unpieced sashing is composed of strips cut in one piece. In its simplest application, short strips separate the blocks in the rows, while longer ones separate the rows of blocks.

Most commonly, the long sashing strips run vertically. The eye is naturally drawn to and follows the vertical line; therefore, you want this line as straight as possible. In addition, the uninterrupted vertical strips help stabilize the quilt top, especially when they are cut on the lengthwise straight grain.

Tip

When planning a quilt with sashing strips, try to arrange it so the sashing falls at the edge of the mattress.

3

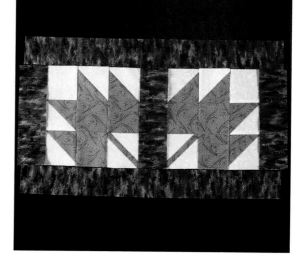

Choice of sashing fabric has a profound impact on the appearance of your quilt. **Bold, bright prints can enliven sleepy blocks, and they make a dramatic statement by forming a strong framework.** Gentle solids and tone-on-tone prints subdue more boisterous blocks, and they generally play a smaller role in the quilt's overall design.

If *sashing strips* are lighter than the blocks, the sashing appears superimposed over the blocks, creating a latticelike effect. By contrast, light seem to float above darker sashing strips.

Tip

Use your design wall to audition a variety of sashing fabrics before making the final selection.

4

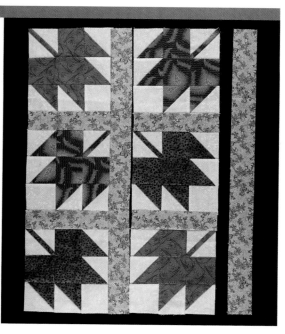

Cut short sashing strips the same length as the unfinished blocks. To calculate the cut length of long sashing strips, first count the number of blocks and sashing strips in a vertical row. **Multiply the finished block size by the number of blocks per row. Then multiply the finished strip width by the number of sashing strips per row. Add the two together and add ½ inch for seam allowances.**

For example, 3 blocks × 12 inches equals 36 inches. And 4 sashing strips × 3 inches equals 12 inches. Cut the vertical sashing strips 48½ inches long (36 plus 12 plus ½ inch for seam allowances).

Tip

Cut sashing strips to calculated measurements, and ease blocks and rows to fit. Do not tailor sashing strips to individual row measurements.

Referring to your quilt diagram, count the number of vertical and horizontal sashing strips needed.

Rotary cut the required number of vertical strips to the width and length desired. **Cut these strips on the lengthwise grain, if possible,** by folding your fabric in half, cut end to cut end, and then in half again.

Determine the number of short horizontal strips that can be cut from a single long strip. **Cut long strips the same width as the vertical sashing, then cut these into the required number of shorter segments.**

Tip

Make sure your ruler lines up perpendicular to both folded edges for a straight sashing strip.

Arrange the blocks and sashing strips; sew them together using the chain-piecing technique described in Steps 5 and 6 of "The ABCs of Settings" on page 23.

Join each assembled row to a long sashing strip, easing to fit if necessary. To ensure that the horizontal seams line up across the sashing strip, **place a ruler along the seam of the horizontal sashing strip. Make a mark on the opposite edge of the vertical sashing strip; match the mark to the cross seams of the next row of blocks.**

Cornerstones add a whole new dimension to your quilt. Add them to your quilt diagram and count the number required.

Cut cornerstones from strips the same width as the sashing strips. Determine how many strips to cut by dividing the strip width (40 to 42 inches) by the cut size of your cornerstones (2¼ inches here). Crosscut the strips into squares.

The vertical and horizontal sashing strips used with the cornerstones are all the same length (finished block size, plus ½ inch).

Tip

For extra punch, try a pieced sashing square. Square within a Square or Nine Patch blocks are easy to piece and work well.

ADDING SASHING TO THE MIX

8

Pieced sashing adds still another dimension to a quilt plan. This easy pieced sashing requires triangles on all four corners of each sashing strip. **If the triangles are the same fabric as the cornerstones, stars twinkle where the sashing strips intersect.**

To construct these sashing strips, measure the *finished* width of the sashing strip. Divide it in half, then add ½ inch for seams. Cut squares for the stars to that dimension. **Draw a diagonal line across the back of the square, align it with a corner of the sashing strip, then stitch on the line.** Trim, then fold the triangle back to the corner.

Tip

A Chaco-liner is great for marking diagonal sewing lines. It shows up on dark fabrics and doesn't stretch the bias as it rolls along.

9

Try multiple strips for the sashing, either equal in size or with narrow strips on the outer edges and a wider one in the middle. Paired with a Nine Patch cornerstone that continues the design, this sashing forms a secondary pattern, thus adding even more movement and excitement to the quilt.

Another variation of the striped sashing is Garden Maze sashing. This requires a pieced cornerstone that is constructed using templates. Draft the unit shown in the photo on graph paper, then make the required templates, adding ¼-inch seam allowances to each shape.

Tip

The traditional Garden Maze sashing is especially effective for floral appliqué blocks.

10

When you include sashing strips in a diagonally set quilt, both the side and corner setting triangles must be cut large enough to accommodate the block and sashing strip together. To determine the size square to cut for side-setting triangles, add the finished block size to the finished sashing strip width. Multiply the new number by 1.414 (the diagonal measurement of the combined pieces). Add 1¼ inches for seam allowances. To find the size square to cut for corner triangles, add the finished block size, plus twice the finished sashing strip width. Multiply by 0.707, then add ⅞ inch for seams.

40

The Quilter's
Problem Solver

Cornerstone Conundrums

Problem	Solution
Not enough fabric for all the cornerstones.	Try using a variety of fabrics for cornerstones. You can repeat several of the colors or fabrics used in the blocks, or you can make them completely scrappy. If you choose the pieced star option when you design the sashing strips and cornerstones, a variety of colors can be especially pleasing.
Cornerstones look too busy.	Try a fabric that is very similar in color and pattern to the sashing strips. This will provide a very subtle difference between the sashing strips and the cornerstones, and it will help calm a busy-feeling quilt.
Plain cornerstones are boring.	A small pieced block or unit from the block used in the quilt makes a great cornerstone. Try a simple Square within a Square, or isolate a unit from the block and use it between the sashing strips.

Skill Builder

Try some of these ideas for creative sashing:

Experiment with striped fabric for sashing strips. Stripes can be cut to run vertically or horizontally. The effects can be dramatic, especially when teamed with simply pieced sashing or cornerstones.

Try sashing of varying widths within the same quilt. This is especially useful when working with different-size blocks, such as workshop or class projects, sewing room experiments, and other orphan blocks.

Cut sashing from the same fabric as the basic block background, and blocks appear to "float," creating a light, airy effect.

Try This!

You can have the illusion of diagonal pieced sashing without complex drafting and piecing. Combine a Nine Patch or similar block with squares that form an X with any other block, using an alternate-block arrangement. If the background of both the basic block and the alternate block is the same, the illusion is even more distinct. Set the blocks diagonally for still another dynamite look.

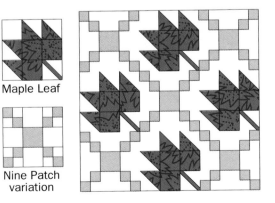

Maple Leaf

Nine Patch variation

ADDING SASHING TO THE MIX

41

Easy
Bar Sets

B ar, or "strippy" quilts have a fresh look that is appealing either on a bed or on a wall. Alternating bars offer a place to show off a beautiful quilting design or add exciting color and pattern with a stunning stripe. Bar quilts can be made with blocks, with natural bar-style patterns (such as Flying Geese or Chinese Coins), or with appliquéd bars. They have an added appeal for busy quilters—since they require fewer blocks to end up with the same size quilt, bar quilts are usually faster to make.

Getting Ready

The *bar* in a bar setting is the pieced section, while the *strip or setting strip* is the fabric between the bars. Solids, prints, and striped fabrics all work well between the pieced bars. If you did not choose fabrics to use for the strips when you made the blocks, select possible choices to audition with your blocks or bars now.

If you are using blocks for your bar rather than a linear pattern, decide whether to set them straight or diagonally between the strips. Straight-set blocks work especially well when they form a secondary pattern where the blocks meet. Diagonal sets, on the other hand, show individual blocks to best advantage. Arrange the blocks on a design wall for a better perspective as you compose the quilt.

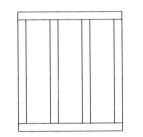

Bar Sets

1 Sketch your planned layout on graph paper. Calculate the width of the bars. If you use diagonally set blocks, use the diagonal measurement to calculate the width of the bar. **The setting strips can be the same width as, or narrower than, the bars.** Determine the number of strips and bars required and the number of blocks or units per bar.

The quilt looks best when you begin and end the design with a bar, and then add borders around the entire quilt. The borders are often the same fabric as the setting strips.

Tip

Try horizontal rather than vertical bars for pictorial motifs or for quilts designed for locations that look best with horizontal lines, such as above sofa backs.

Choose fabrics for the setting strip that will enhance the pieced bar. A solid fabric works best if you want to do elaborate quilting. Repeating a print fabric used in the pattern or using the same fabric as the background or the triangles of bars can create interesting visual illusions. Strips of striped fabric provide a dramatic showcase for the bar and reinforce the linear design of the quilt. **Audition the various choices on your design wall to see which option works best.**

Tip

Traditional Amish bar quilt designs are composed of solid-color strips with no pieced bars between them. These can showcase intricate quilting designs.

3

Press the bars carefully. Check to be sure that they are all the same length. If they are not, trim or block them as necessary.

Cut setting strips the required width and 1 or 2 inches longer than required to allow for trimming. Cut them on the lengthwise grain if possible. **Lay out a bar on your cutting surface or on the floor. Arrange up to four strips, all stacked together, on the bar. Smooth the strips and the bar, then trim both ends of the strips to match the bar.** Trim the remaining strips so they are all the same length.

Tip

If you prefer to measure the bar, use a metal tape measure to get the most accurate measurement. Cloth or vinyl tape measures can stretch.

4

Fold each setting strip in half lengthwise, then in quarters. Press the fold lines, or place a pin at each fold line. Do the same with each pieced bar, marking the folds with pins rather than pressing them. Be sure to mark both edges of both the strips and the borders.

To assemble the quilt, match the ends, centers, and quarter marks of a setting strip and a bar. Pin the matched points together, then pin the remainder of the strip at frequent intervals. Stitch the strip to the bar.

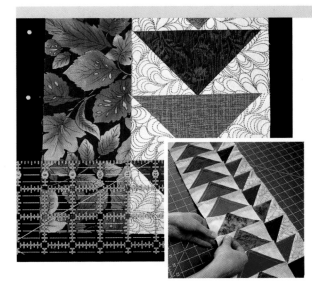

To ensure that the patterns of the bars align evenly on both sides of the setting strips, mark the placement of the seams on the opposite edge of the strip. **Pin the next bar unit to the strip, matching the seam intersections to the markings on the strip.** Stitch the bar to the strip.

Add the next strip, then repeat the marking and pinning to complete the quilt top.

Tip

Stitch in the same direction on both sides of the strip to avoid twisting the fabric.

A pieced setting strip may work best with your bar quilt. Piecing the strip enables you to add more color, widen a striped fabric to a required width, or **make your own striped fabric if you can't find one that you like. Assemble the strip-pieced stripe, then trim it to fit.**

Tip

Appliquéd designs, particularly vines, would look wonderful between two narrow strips.

To construct a bar with diagonal blocks, you will need half-square triangles for the corners of each bar and quarter-square triangles between the blocks.

Refer to "The Basics of Diagonal Sets" on page 30 for triangle cutting directions. **Stitch two half-square triangles on the upper sides of the first block and a quarter-square triangle on the lower right side. Sew quarter-square triangles to the upper left and lower right sides of the next block.** Stitch the units together, ending with half-square triangle corners on the last block.

Tip

Each bar requires four half-square triangles, but you must count the number of quarter-square triangles required.

EASY BAR SETS

45

Dynamic
Zigzag Sets

The zigzag set is not subtle; it vibrates with energy and calls out for attention. There's no question why this set is also called Streak of Lightning! A less-commonly used setting, it is characterized by its bold zigzagging lines and frequently adventurous use of brightly colored fabrics for the setting pieces. This is a particularly good setting for oddly shaped blocks, such as the triangular Sugar Loaf, or for a group of scrappy blocks, but any block can become a candidate simply by being set diagonally.

Getting Ready

What You'll Need

Completed quilt blocks

¼" or ⅛" graph paper and pencil

Fabric for triangles

Rotary cutter and mat

6" × 24" rotary ruler

15" square rotary ruler

Calculator

Pins

Sewing machine

Thread

Thread snips

Zigzag settings are a terrific solution for blocks that don't fit into a standard side-by-side or sashed arrangement. There is usually a way to fit these blocks all into a zigzag set and make them look good. This setting is also great for blocks that look best on point or for a group of otherwise unrelated blocks.

Designs that form secondary patterns when placed side by side are not the best choice for this set, though. Side triangles interrupt the side-by-side setting and disrupt the pattern flow.

This set is most successful when there is high contrast between the blocks and the setting fabric, so think about value in addition to color when making fabric choices. Bright setting fabrics will make the zigzags stand out, while more neutral fabrics make the blocks appear to float.

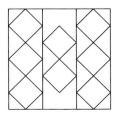

Zigzag Sets

Sketch your proposed quilt on graph paper. Arrange the blocks in an uneven number of vertical rows. The even rows should contain one block fewer than the odd rows. **The blocks in each vertical row should be placed on point, with their corners touching. The blocks in the odd-numbered rows should line up across the quilt.** Move the blocks in the even-numbered rows so they are offset by half a block.

Add half-square triangles to each corner of each odd-numbered row, then add quarter-square triangles in the remaining spaces.

Tip

Consider half blocks to fill in the top and bottom of each even-numbered row in the set.

2

If you prefer half-blocks for the even-numbered rows, you must be sure to allow for ¼-inch-wide seams on all sides. There are two ways to handle these blocks.

You can draft and construct half-blocks that include the seam allowance. Draft the full block on graph paper, then draw a line diagonally across it. Draw another line ¼ inch from the diagonal line. Use the pattern pieces to make templates or to determine rotary-cutting dimensions.

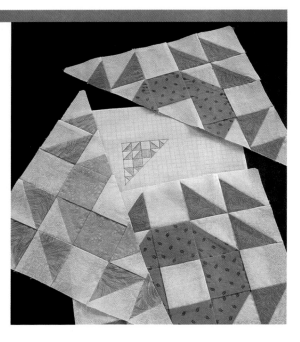

3

Cut the triangles for the sides and corners so the outer edge of the row is on the straight grain. For the side triangles, this means that the longest side must be on the straight grain, while for the corner triangles, the shorter sides must be on the straight grain.

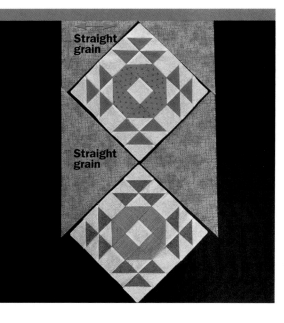

Straight grain

Straight grain

4

To cut the side-setting triangles, determine the finished measurement of the block (actual size, less ½ inch for seams). Multiply the finished size by 1.414 to find the diagonal measurement and round it up to the nearest ¼ inch. Add 1¼ inches for seam allowances, then cut a square that size. **Cut the square along both diagonals for four side-setting triangles that each have the straight grain on their long edges.**

Determining the size of the corner triangles also requires that you know the finished measurement of the block. This time, multiply it by 0.707, round it up to the nearest ¼ inch, and then add ⅞ inch. **Cut a square of the setting fabric that size, then cut it along one diagonal for two corner triangles.** You will need four of these triangles for each odd-numbered row of your zigzag set quilt.

Tip

Cut the side and corner triangles about 1" larger than necessary, and trim them after you sew the row together for a perfect fit.

To assemble the rows, sew the triangles to the blocks in diagonal rows. Add the corner blocks. Because the edges of the triangles that you are sewing are all bias edges, be sure to sew with the triangle on the bottom. This helps prevent the bias edge from stretching. Sew the diagonal rows of blocks and triangles together to complete each vertical row.

To assemble the rows, first mark the center point of each side-setting triangle. **Pin the rows together, matching the corner of the block in one row to the center of the side triangle in the next row.**

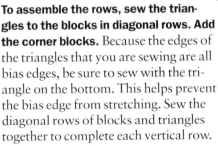

Some blocks naturally form zigzag sets. A block that is divided diagonally with one side pieced and the other side an unpieced triangle makes a perfect candidate for a zigzag set. Set these blocks in a straight side-by-side set with pairs of plain triangles facing each other. Offset the block placement in each row by one block and the result will be a chevron or zigzag pattern.

Tip

You can create zigzag sets with blocks that are completely pieced, too. Blocks with strong diagonals, like Log Cabins, make terrific zigzag quilts.

DYNAMIC ZIGZAG SETS

Designing
Medallion Sets

This elegant set has a classic, time-honored place in our quiltmaking history. Some of the first quilts made by our foremothers were done in the medallion style. But more than that, a medallion set is fun. This is your chance to make one spectacular block and then play with variations on its theme in a series of borders. There's no boredom in this set, since it changes with every border. Working with the medallion set might even sharpen design skills you may not have known you had. So, colored pencils to the ready—let's begin!

Getting Ready

A medallion quilt starts with one notable block, worthy of a solo spotlight, or several less complex blocks stitched together for the center. The borders will build on the colors and shapes in the central block, so select coordinating fabrics with a variety of scales, textures, and values for these areas. Do some preliminary planning on graph paper to ensure that the proportions of the quilt and the scale of the borders are pleasing. Think about adding plain or appliqué borders to give the eye a place to rest or to make the pieced borders fit.

Although you might alter your original plan as you proceed, it will help you work out your ideas and it will function as a design guide.

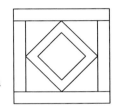

Completed block or blocks for center

Fabric for borders

¼" or ⅛" graph paper and pencil

Colored pencils

Rotary cutter and mat

6" × 24" rotary ruler

Pins

Sewing machine

Thread

Thread snips

Center Options

Many potential medallion centers are more interesting when they are placed diagonally. The triangles that form the corners of a diagonal center give the eye a place to rest before moving to the surrounding borders. They also provide a larger space for beautiful quilting or for an appliqué design. Diagonally set blocks may be framed with one or more borders before corner triangles are added.

Tip

Cut the corner triangles extra large to allow the center design to float inside the borders.

D E S I G N I N G   M E D A L L I O N   S E T S

2

Several blocks that form an interesting secondary design are also a good choice for the center of a medallion set. Set them side by side, then rotate the blocks a quarter-turn around the center to see which arrangement is more dynamic. Try setting the individual blocks diagonally, or set the assembled blocks on point for another look.

Tip

Many other traditional designs form interesting new patterns when their background shapes are extended beyond the block.

3

Background shapes that repeat into the border can expand a fairly simple block and complete a partial pattern.

In the example shown, a simple star design is surrounded with a border of background fabric. The triangles between the star points are repeated in the center of the borders, and the Four Patch units continue into the corners of the block. By playing with the color placement, a totally new star pattern, appropriate for a medallion center, emerges.

4

Central medallions need not be square. Try designing blocks in other shapes, such as octagons, hexagons, circles, and other star shapes. Play with your center design to explore all the possibilities.

A less formal medallion quilt can start with several less complex blocks set straight, rather than diagonally. For example, four house blocks can star in the center of a folk style quilt, with simple pieced borders surrounding it.

Border Ideas

Sketch proposed border outlines on your graph paper. It isn't necessary to draw in the precise border design, just the width and placement. Vary the width of borders, and take care that they do not overpower the center in either size or number. **A narrow border between two wider ones not only provides an accent, but it also stabilizes the pieced borders and helps prevent them from stretching.** This is particularly valuable if you cut some of the fabrics in the adjacent border off-grain to take advantage of a printed pattern.

Tip

A plain border between the center design and a pieced border, or between two pieced borders, makes the borders easier to fit.

Border designs should relate both to each other and to the center. Repeating some of the shapes or units from the center design is a clever way to integrate the borders and the center design.

Plan pieced borders so the design is complete on each side and all four corners are identical. **If a pieced border doesn't turn the corner naturally, you may break it in the middle and construct it in a mirror image for the second half.**

Tip

Take a Polaroid photo of the quilt after each border is added to gain perspective on the composition.

Striped fabrics make wonderful borders for medallion quilts. Several fabric manufacturers print complex stripes that are appropriate for borders. One way to plan how to turn the corner with stripes is to use mitered corners. (See "Perfectly Mitered Borders" on page 80.) **Arrange the striped border so that designs meet in a pleasing way at the corners. Fold the fabric at several different places to find the best mitered corner design.**

Sometimes patterns in a striped fabric border don't meet exactly at the corners. If this happens, cut the borders long enough to match the corners, then take small tucks in the stripe at inconspicuous spots along its length to fit.

Tip

A mirror placed at a 45 degree angle to the striped fabric will show how the pattern turns the corner.

DESIGNING MEDALLION SETS

4

To create a rectangular medallion quilt, you can start with a rectangular center. Try piecing multiple blocks to form a rectangle, or redesign a block into a rectangular shape. Or you can add a border to just the top and bottom of the center design and omit the side borders.

In the design shown, the top and bottom strips intersect the outer corner of the central design, while the side strips intersect several inches from the corner, thus turning a square design into a rectangular quilt.

5

Tip

Pin borders carefully before sewing so that the same design elements are in the same positions on all sides of the quilt.

Each time you add a border, check that the corners are square by aligning them with a large ruler and trimming them if necessary. Also, make sure that the sides are straight and equal in length. You can check this easily by folding the quilt in half lengthwise and aligning the sides. Check the top and bottom edges by folding the quilt crosswise. Correct any discrepancies before you add the next border. Block the quilt, adjust the seams, or carefully trim the piece. An uncorrected problem compounds as you add subsequent borders.

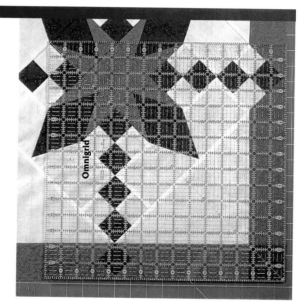

6

Tip

Let appliquéd shapes "spill over" into plain or pieced areas for a less formal, somewhat whimsical look.

Combine piecing and appliqué to enhance both techniques. Stunning quilts can be created with an appliqué center and pieced borders, a pieced center with appliqué borders, or a mixture of pieced and appliquéd borders and setting triangles. And, of course, the entire quilt can be appliquéd. The key to a successful combination of piecing and appliqué is continuity of color and design.

The Quilter's Problem Solver

Layering and Basting Medallion Quilts

Problem	Solution
Borders became distorted when they were layered.	Use a ruler as a guide to straighten each border seam. Make sure the corners are square as you smooth the quilt top on the batting and backing. A large, square rotary ruler will help with this process. Pin along the entire border seam with straight pins before basting it.
Quilt stretches as it is placed in the hoop.	Baste with smaller and slightly tighter stitches so that the layers do not pull out of alignment as the quilt is handled during quilting. You may want to baste this style of quilt a bit more closely than you normally do. This is especially important if you are using a small frame. Quilt in the ditch along the border seams before quilting within the border. This will both define the border and anchor it.

Skill Builder

Piece borders on paper foundations for a perfect fit every time. Many border patterns can be pieced with one foundation per side; break longer or more complex ones into segments.

To prepare multiple foundations, trace the design onto one foundation. Layer the rest of the papers (up to 12 segments) and sew along all the lines of the design with an unthreaded sewing machine.

If the paper isn't long enough for the entire border, overlap sections as you sew. Leave the foundation in place until the next border is added.

Try This!

Learn about medallion sets and stretch your quiltmaking and designing skills by organizing a Round Robin with four or five friends. Each member constructs a center for the medallion. The quilts are rotated to each member in turn; each one adds a border. The border additions usually have some requirements, such as including a specific shape. When all borders are complete, the quilt is returned to the person who made the center. To avoid creative bottlenecks, set a time limit for the completion of each step in the Round Robin.

DESIGNING MEDALLION SETS

55

Twist 'n Turn
Sets

A re you trying to figure out what to do with a group of blocks that aren't quite the same size? Or maybe you have some that need a little pizzazz? Try Sharyn Craig's fresh, new twist method to make them all match or to add that needed sparkle. Her "Twist 'n Turn" block framing technique provides an easy and forgiving way to whimsically arrange the blocks, with a unique quilt setting as the pleasing result.

Getting Ready

This method works best with blocks that differ in size by 1 inch or less. If they differ by more, use wider strips for the smaller blocks. The ultimate goal is to make all the framed blocks the same size.

Choose lots of different fabrics for framing strips. Audition your choices by arranging them around the blocks in the twist style before actually cutting fabric. Selecting similar values for the four triangles that frame any one block is more important than the actual color selected. The framing pieces around any one block can be all the same fabric or four totally different fabrics.

Cut strips either 2½ or 3½ inches wide (your choice) from the framing fabrics. To give yourself enough choices, cut plenty of strips—at least two for each block. Save the leftovers for other projects.

What You'll Need

- **Completed quilt blocks**
- **Assorted fabric strips 2½" or 3½" wide**
- **Rotary cutter and mat**
- **6" × 24" rotary ruler**
- **9½" or larger square rotary ruler**
- **Pins**
- **Sewing machine**
- **Thread**
- **Thread snips**
- **Iron and ironing board**

Twist 'n Turn

Measure the block from raw edge to raw edge. Add 5½ inches to this number to determine the size of the rectangles to cut for the twist pieces. For example, our block measures 6½ inches square. When we add 5½ inches, the total is 12 inches. We will use this measurement to cut rectangles from our strips.

Tip

Square blocks, rather than rectangular ones, work best for this set.

2

Select four framing strips, all the same width. Fold the strips in half, wrong sides together, matching the selvages. Stack the four folded strips one on top of another with the selvages together. **Trim off the selvages, then cut rectangles the length you determined in Step 1 on page 57.**

3

Align the edge of your ruler with two opposite corners of the stack of rectangles, then cut along the edge of the ruler to create long triangles. The triangles you have cut will yield blocks twisting both to the right and to the left. It doesn't matter which diagonal you cut. Since your fabrics are folded, you'll automatically have pairs of opposite triangles.

Tip

If the strips are all placed right side up and the rectangles cut in the same direction, the blocks will all twist the same way.

4

Separate the resulting triangles and arrange them into four groups. Each group should have one triangle of each color, and all the triangles in a group should have their right-angle corners in the same position. If you lay the triangles on the cutting mat with the skinny point of the triangle toward you, it will become immediately obvious whether the triangle is a right corner or a left corner. There are enough triangles to frame four blocks.

Tip

Triangles with corners on the right twist the block to the right. Triangles with corners on the left twist the block to the left.

Choose a block and one set of triangles with the square corner on the left. Position the first triangle on top of the block, right sides together, matching the square corner of the triangle with the corner of the block. **Starting at the square corner, stitch along the edge, ending the seam approximately halfway to the corner.** This first seam is always a partial seam. Press the seam toward the triangle.

Tip

When adding triangles with square corners on the right, sew with the block on top. When adding triangles with square corners on the left, sew with the triangle on top.

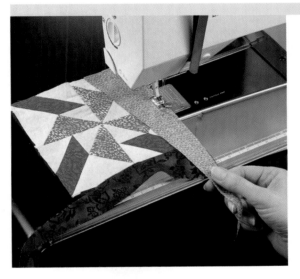

Arrange the second triangle on the block as shown, again matching the square corner of the triangle with the corner of the block. The narrow point of the triangle will cross the short edge of the previous triangle. Stitch the entire seam, then press the seam allowance toward the triangle.

Tip

Don't worry about the point of the triangle that extends beyond the edge of the block. Trim it off when you square up the block.

Add the two remaining triangles, one at a time, in the same manner. Press the seam allowance toward the triangle after each addition. **After the fourth triangle is sewn on, finish sewing the partial seam.**

Carefully press the block. There is a slight bias grain on the outside edge of the block, and pressing well now, before you square up the block, will help tame the bias and keep it from being a problem. Be careful not to pull on the outer edges as you press, as this will stretch and distort the block.

Tip

Spray the blocks with Magic Sizing or spray starch, then press to help keep the bias edges in check.

T W I S T ' N   T U R N   S E T S

To square up the block, position one corner of a square ruler on the seam line in the upper right corner. **Twist and manipulate the ruler so the same measurement appears at the seam line on the remaining three corners.** This is your magic number. *The ruler will not be parallel to the edges of the block.* Trim the right and top edges.

The magic number for our sample block is 8 inches. Notice that the 8-inch measurement intersects all seam lines except the upper right.

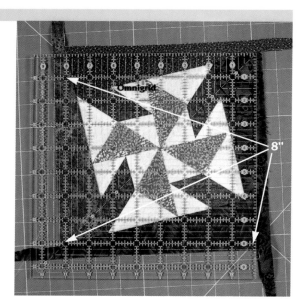

Square the block as large as possible. You can always cut the block down to a smaller size if it becomes necessary.

Rotate the block and arrange the ruler so your magic number is on the trimmed corner. **Align the adjacent edges of the ruler with the trimmed edges of the block, and trim the two remaining sides (left and bottom edges).** If you are left-handed, begin in the upper left corner of the block. **Square all the remaining blocks to the same size.**

The framed blocks look great either set side by side or with sashing strips and setting squares. Sashing adds another color dimension, and it can make the quilt larger without making extra blocks.

Or try this special effect, without having to add sashing pieces. **Use only two different fabrics, and place them on opposite sides of each block. Then, when you rotate the blocks on the design wall, a four-pointed star appears where the blocks come together.** Be careful, though, that the star doesn't overpower the blocks.

The Quilter's
Problem Solver

Tricks with Twists

Problem	Solution
Blocks are puckered and uneven.	Carefully press the blocks before framing them. A steam iron can work miracles at this stage of the game. If the blocks are really uneven, you may want to square them up before you frame them, even if it makes them a bit smaller to start with.
Difference in blocks is more than 1 inch.	Frame the smaller blocks with wider strips and the larger blocks with narrower strips. There's no rule that says all the framing strips have to be the same size.

Skill Builder

Try a double or even a triple twist! This gives you even more opportunity to play with color in the framing.

If your blocks are very different in size you might want to single twist some, double twist some, and even triple twist others.

Do all the blocks have to be twisted? No! You could leave some blocks untwisted. The goal is to create a quilt where the blocks relate, lie flat, go together easily, and look good. You have permission to accomplish that with any method you wish.

Try This!

For your first blocks, 2½-inch and 3½-inch strips are suggested. But feel free to use other strip widths in the process.

If you prefer another strip width, cut only enough for one block to begin with. You may have to adjust the 5½-inch add-on amount, because it reflects the height of the triangle and the points that result from bisecting a rectangle. The narrower you cut the strip, the more length you must allow to be sure that there is enough seam allowance for trimming the blocks. When you cut narrow strips, cut them 6 to 8 inches longer than the block size. When you cut wider (4 to 5 inches wide) strips, the additional length is not as crucial; add 5½ inches as described on page 57.

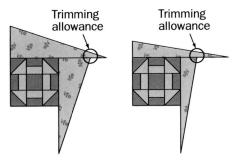

Trimming allowance   Trimming allowance

TWIST 'N TURN SETS

61

Remember the jigsaw puzzles you put together as a child and how exciting it was to get all the pieces to fit together? You can do the same thing with quilts, too. You can choose one block pattern, make it in several different sizes, then fit all the pieces together; or you can assemble orphan blocks, assorted parts of blocks, and fabric scraps. You'll soon learn to see connections between shapes, colors, and sizes that will make all your quilt-making more interesting. This is your chance to play again—and this time you make the rules.

Getting Ready

Gather all your orphan blocks, the ones left over from projects you have completed or those that didn't quite work as intended. Also, collect the miscellaneous triangle squares, Flying Geese, Nine Patch units, and other small pieces you have been saving. Chose fabrics to accompany the blocks. Select compatible colors in several values and a variety of scales and textures.

Determine the dominant mood of your collected items. Puzzle quilts can have many different moods, from casual and scrappy to calm and sophisticated. The mood is established by the blocks you are working with, the fabric you add as connector pieces, and the composition.

If you prefer, you can make a variety of blocks and filler units specifically for your puzzle quilt. In this case, assemble some block ideas and a wide variety of fabrics that fit the mood you desire.

Puzzle Sets

1

Place your blocks on a design wall in a pleasing arrangement. Don't be concerned with creating rows of blocks—arrange them by the colors and shapes in the block. Mix up the block sizes. A reducing glass, which makes the wall look farther away, makes it easier to see if the pieces are balanced.

If there are empty spaces around the blocks, don't worry. You can fill them with miscellaneous bits and pieces. Don't even consider construction methods yet; these will come later. Just let yourself go and play with various block arrangements.

Tip

Substitute the viewfinder of a camera for a reducing glass, or look through the "wrong" end of binoculars.

CLEVER PUZZLE SETS

2

Draw your block arrangement on graph paper. This will serve several purposes. It will give you a map to help work out the sizes and shapes of connector strips, small pieced units, and other blocks, if you want to use them. It will also provide a record of where you started. If you move blocks to try other arrangements, you can get back to where you started by checking your map.

Tip

Take a Polaroid photo of each arrangement so you can recreate the one you like best.

3

Fill in some of the smaller spaces between the blocks with strips of several fabrics of the same color. A variety of background fabrics seems to work well in this capacity.

For the ultimate scrappy quilt with an antique look, fit the blocks together with no connector strips or blocks. This becomes a real jigsaw puzzle if your blocks are different sizes and shapes.

4

Pieced fill-in strips and blocks can maintain the scrappy look while they make it easier to fit blocks together. Try repeating shapes from the blocks as fill-in pieces to provide a unified look.

Some familiar, easily pieced units also work well as connector pieces. **Flying Geese, Nine Patch units, Pinwheels, or Crazy-pieced blocks all work well.** Plain squares or rectangles appliquéd with simple designs add extra pizzazz to puzzle quilts.

Tip

If you're unsure about a block arrangement, leave it on your design wall overnight. You'll see it with a fresh perspective in the morning.

Don't be afraid to cut up blocks and use the pieces to fill in spaces in your design. There's no rule that says a block, once constructed, must stay whole. Cut shapes as required to fit the holes in your design, or just cut blocks apart and stitch them together in a different arrangement. You can come up with some interesting patterns using this technique.

If you've modified your quilt layout from your graph paper drawing, sketch your new layout. Although it is not necessary to draw in each piece of each pattern, sketch in enough to easily identify each block or unit. Then, if the blocks get mixed up, it will be easier to rearrange them.

To determine the best way to construct the quilt top, divide the quilt into sections that you can easily sew together into units. Mark them with a dark pen or pencil.

Tip

Working out the construction order before you start stitching will help reduce the number of set-in seams required.

Press seams as you construct each unit. Before the final assembly, block and press each unit. **The pressing order will depend on the placement of the seams, but pressing seams open where possible will help the quilt lie flat and will make the quilting easier.**

CLEVER PUZZLE SETS

8

Create a theme quilt with appliqué blocks made specifically to fit with the chosen subject. Themes such as holidays, hobbies, or favorite decorating motifs all make delightful puzzle quilts. **If you are making blocks specifically for the quilt, choose a variety of fabrics for both the backgrounds and the blocks. Mix and match the fabrics and coordinate them with the connector blocks and strips.**

9

If all the blocks in a puzzle quilt are a size that is the multiple of a chosen number, the blocks will be easier to fit together because the sizes are predetermined and work together. You can use individual units from the blocks to make the smaller connector pieces, without modifying or redrafting the cut sizes of your pieces. The result can be lots of options for interesting compositions. For example, quilts based on a 3-inch multiple would make it possible to use 3-inch, 6-inch, 9-inch, and 12-inch blocks. Those based on a 4-inch multiple can contain 4-inch, 8-inch, 12-inch, and 16-inch blocks.

10

Tip

When making a modular quilt with the same block design, make fabric paste-ups to see the effect of color placement on the pattern.

Make the same block pattern in several sizes for a sophisticated look. You can use the same fabrics in the same positions in all the blocks, or you can rearrange the placement of the fabrics within the blocks. **Try using different prints in the same colors, or make the blocks totally scrappy. Arrange the different-size blocks randomly,** or make the sizes increase or decrease in a regular pattern across the quilt top. The possibilities are limited only by your imagination!

The Quilter's Problem Solver

Filling the Holes

Problem	Solution
Connector unit doesn't quite fit.	Make a connector unit that you already have fit by adding strips to one or two sides, then trimming it to fit the space. Don't forget to add seam allowances. Or appliqué some simple shapes on a piece of fabric that fits the space.
Unfilled spaces are an odd size.	Measure the space that needs to be filled. Remember to calculate the finished size, without seam allowances. Draw the shape on graph paper, then draft a simple connector shape, such as a Pinwheel or a Square within a Square, on the graph paper. Make templates if necessary to construct the units, or try making over-size units and trimming them to fit. Use folded corners to construct the Square within a Square block. See Step 5 of "Easy & Creative Pieced Borders," page 98.

Pinwheel   Square within a Square

Pieced Borders," page 98.

Skill Builder

For a guild activity, collect orphan blocks from guild members. Divide the blocks into sets by color, and pass the sets out to individuals or teams for a puzzle quilt challenge. Plan a work day with various members of a team assigned to composition, cutting and designing connector strips, sewing, and pressing. Rotate the jobs several times during the day. This is a wonderful way to learn from each other and, by working quickly, to stifle creative inhibitions!

Try This!

Puzzle quilts are a fine way to expand your horizons. Don't be too quick to settle on an arrangement. Play with some of these variations to see if you find a creative surprise or two:

❑ Create a low-contrast background with string or crazy piecing and appliqué the blocks randomly over the surface.

❑ Use some of the blocks for a border, or overlap some blocks into the border.

❑ Cut up and repiece some of the blocks with strips between the sections.

CLEVER PUZZLE SETS

Exploring Different
Border Options

A border deserves to be more than an afterthought. The best way to create a dynamic border to frame your quilt is to plan for it right from the start. The very best borders enhance the center design area and give the viewer's eye a natural place to stop at the outer edge. A good border emphasizes the primary design without stealing center stage. To help you create a border that is the perfect finishing touch, take a look at the different border styles presented on the following pages.

Getting Ready

What You'll Need

Quilt top

¼" or ⅛" graph paper and pencil

Colored pencils

Ruler

Quilt books with photos of borders for inspiration

You've got a quilt top almost completed, and it's time to plan how to finish it. Think about size—are you making a quilt for a specific wall space or for a particular bed? If you like to quilt, you might like a wide border on which to show off hand or machine quilting. Or maybe you'd prefer to do more piecing or appliquéing to reach the appropriate size, then finish with a smaller border?

The body of a bed quilt usually covers the top of the mattress; the "drop" can be all border, or some of the main part of the quilt with a border. Ultimately, the proportion of quilt to border becomes a personal preference, keeping in mind that very narrow or very wide borders can look out of place. Consider the impact of the whole quilt as you plan. Look at quilts everywhere: in books, in homes, at shows, and in antique shops to get ideas for your final edge.

Border Styles

Plain Borders

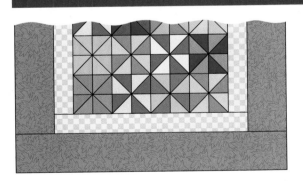

Unpieced borders are cut either from fabrics that are used in the body of the quilt or that will coordinate with them. A light fabric, which is often used with appliquéd designs, gives an airy look to the quilt, while a dark or dark-medium value border provides a strong frame. **Multiple strips of several of the fabrics from the quilt sewn together make an excellent frame, providing continuity of color and texture.** Use different widths for these multiple borders, graduating from narrow to wide, or narrow to wide and back to narrow.

Tip

Choose a commanding bright or dark fabric for a narrow (¼" to ⅜" wide) inner border.

Straight Corners

Butted corners require the least amount of fabric and are the simplest way of dealing with corners. The most common construction method is to add the side borders first, then the top and bottom so they overlap the side borders.

Adding corner squares takes butted borders a step further. They provide a second color focus within the border, helping move your eye from the center to the edges of the quilt. While plain corner squares are traditionally used with many designs, a pieced block design or an element from the quilt can also be used as a corner square.

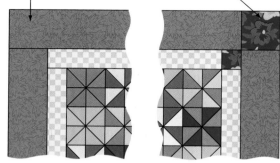

Butted border   Corner square

Mitered Borders

Tip

If you are using multiple plain borders, stitch the border strips together before you add them to the quilt, then miter the corners.

Mitered corners are more complex, use a little more fabric, and are considered a finer, more formal finish. They are used on quilts that have strong diagonal lines in the block designs. Mitered corners provide a graceful way to enhance the flow of the border design and the quilting design around the corners.

Multiple borders with mitered corners are impressive. All the miters must meet precisely, forming 45 degree angles at the corner.

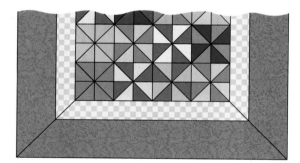

Pieced Borders

Pieced borders add an entirely new dimension to a quilt. **There are many fairly simple, basic patterns and shapes you can choose from, such as Checkerboard and Flying Geese,** or you can select a shape used in the quilt blocks and incorporate it into the border design. Even traditional quilt blocks can be included in this category. Imagine a row of blocks around a quilt and the emphatic statement they can make.

You can make pieced borders fit more easily by adding plain borders that function as spacer strips between borders or between the quilt and the border.

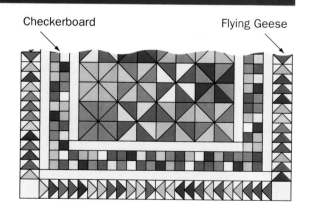

Checkerboard   Flying Geese

Strip-Pieced Borders

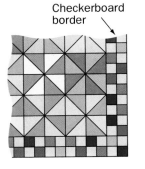

Checkerboard border

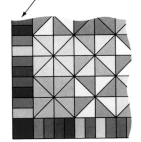

Strippy border

Checkerboard patterns are easily strip pieced. **Use Four Patch or Nine Patch units singly or in more complex arrangements.** Spacer strips between the quilt and the border or between the block units make the borders easier to fit.

Strippy or "piano-key" borders are constructed with short strips sewn together along their long edges. They may be cut in identical or random widths, and they may be positioned perpendicular to or at an angle to the quilt. The angle can change direction at the center of each side, or it can stay the same along each edge.

Use strips of all the fabrics in the quilt to make attractive strippy borders. Add spacer strips to separate them from the block design.

Sawtooth Borders

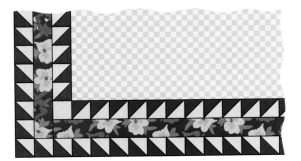

Triangle squares arranged along the edges of a quilt form a Sawtooth design. These triangle squares can be easily mass-produced with quick-piecing techniques. You can even combine several sizes of Sawtooth units to make larger intricate patterns. Since this is a directional pattern, you must decide whether the triangles will march around the quilt in one direction, or whether they will change direction at the corners or in the middle of each side. Most commonly, they change direction in the middle of each side.

Flying Geese Borders

Strips of rectangular Flying Geese units make emphatic borders, and they can be used singly, in multiples, and in different sizes. Like Sawtooth designs, they are directional and may change direction at the corners or in the center of the side. Traditionally, Flying Geese units are twice as wide as they are high, for example 2 × 4 inches or 2½ × 5 inches.

Strips of off-center or crazy Flying Geese are a whimsical alternative to traditional Flying Geese units.

EXPLORING DIFFERENT BORDER OPTIONS

Diamond Borders

Diamond and parallelogram shapes are easily adaptable for use in border designs. Although cutting and piecing these shapes is a little more complicated, they form dynamic patterns when assembled. With either shape, you can use Seminole strip-piecing techniques to avoid cutting and sewing many small pieces.

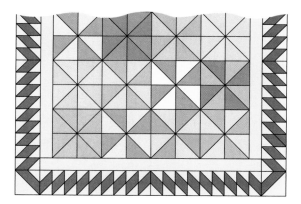

Blocks As Borders

Full blocks (or sections of blocks) from the body of the quilt can be used effectively in the borders. **Place individual block designs in the corners or in the center of each side.** Sometimes these block designs can help complete a pattern in the main body of the quilt.

It is also possible to build-in borders or parts of borders as the quilt is constructed. Coloring blocks or partial blocks in a different way can make them look like borders. Using a darker value fabric for the background is one way to achieve this effect.

Appliquéd Borders

Appliquéd borders are appropriate on both pieced and appliquéd quilts. **The curves, swags, and vines can tie center designs to the outer edge, as well as provide pleasing contrast with the geometric regularity of pieced designs.** While they are most often worked on plain strips, they offer an exciting contrast when stitched over a pieced background.

The Quilter's
Problem Solver

Determining Borders

Problem	Solution
Not sure how many borders are best.	Pin folded pieces of fabric next to your quilt to audition both the number of fabrics and fabric choices for the borders. Stand back and evaluate the effect the borders have on the design. Try different widths and combinations of fabrics. Construct a section of a pieced border using one of the elements and test its effect. Always consider at least two borders. The addition of a narrow inner line of color will frame the other borders. There isn't one right answer; the best choice is always what will enhance the overall effect of your quilt.
Don't know how to determine the best width for a border.	If the size requirements for your quilt allow, plan for a border that is the width of one block or unit of the quilt. Study the effect; try slightly wider or narrower. If you are using a pieced border, the pattern may affect the proportion of border to quilt.

Don't neglect the outer edge. The binding is the final border touch, and it is an important part of the design.

If you want an extra frame, consider using a color from the quilt, perhaps the one you used as a narrow inner border. If the border is complex and ends with a plain strip, use the same fabric for binding. Or try a pieced binding, using fabrics from the quilt. This brings the viewer's eye all the way to the edge and helps tie the whole quilt together.

Try This!

Adding an appliquéd border to a pieced quilt is often a clever strategy. Juxtaposing curves with straight edges and sharp points can be a very effective design technique. Indented areas in the pieced design are a natural place for curved vines or swags. Fabrics with subtle contrasts in value on the underlying pieced border provide the best base for the appliqué design.

Correspondingly, pieced border designs, such as those discussed in this chapter, serve to frame the curves of appliquéd border patterns beautifully.

Simple Borders
with Butted Corners

Your blocks are finally stitched together—now all they need is a border. Plain borders, made from printed or solid fabrics, are the simplest and easiest way to enclose the body of a quilt. Although they are sometimes given less status than the more complicated pieced or appliquéd borders, plain borders are a great frame for an intricate center design, especially one with lots of movement. Borders can emphasize colors or patterns, or they can add a subtle echo of elements in the design. Your choice of fabrics can make the difference between a ho-hum quilt and one that knocks your socks off.

Getting Ready

Planning the border is one of the last creative decisions you face before your quilt top is finished. The width will depend on the finished quilt size needed, but the total border should be no wider than the blocks. Use a multiple of the block size to maintain visual balance. For example, if your blocks are 8 inches, try a 6-inch border (2 is the multiple). If you choose more than one border, make them different widths to avoid a repetitive look. Using the 8-inch block example, one border could be 2 inches and the other 4 inches. Select several fabrics or combinations to audition. Fold them so they are about the same width as the planned border, and lay them against the quilt top. Consider adding an accent color in the form of corner squares.

Cutting and Adding Borders

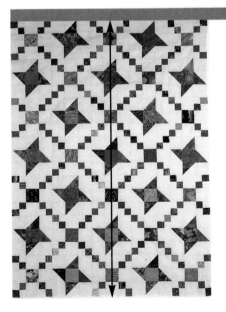

For the minimal-math way to calculate borders, take a rough measurement of the length through the center of the quilt. Even if the directions you are following specify a length for the border, your "real-life" measurement may be different. Add at least 2 inches to the measurement you take. Decide whether you want to cut border strips from the length or the width of the fabric. Although borders cut along the lengthwise grain have no seams and stretch a little less than those cut on the crosswise grain, borders cut crosswise require a lot less fabric.

2

To cut borders accurately along the lengthwise grain of the fabric, fold the fabric cut-end to cut-end. Align the selvages and make sure there are no ripples along the fold. Fold it again so you have four layers. **Align the edge of a square ruler on the left side along the fold and just inside the selvage. Place the long ruler on the left side of the square ruler, pressing them together tightly.** Remove the square ruler. Cut along the edge to remove the selvage. Measure the width of your border, then cut strips as required.

3

If you are using directionally printed fabric, it can be more pleasing to cut the top and bottom borders across the fabric width rather than along the length. **If you must piece strips together to reach the appropriate length, sew the seams straight across the strip and press the seam allowances open.** Take particular care to match stripes, plaids, and large floral motifs whenever possible.

Some quilters feel that sewing the strips together with a diagonal seam makes the seam less visible. See "Try This!" on page 79 for directions for diagonal seams.

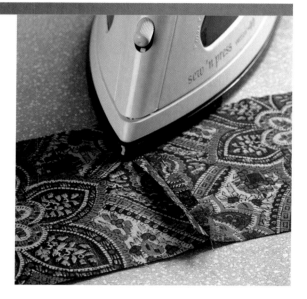

4

To trim borders to size, lay the quilt on your cutting table or an ironing board, and smooth it in place. Arrange the side border strips along the center of the length of the quilt, allowing the excess to extend beyond the top and bottom edges of the quilt. Smooth them in place. **Fold larger quilts in half; fold the border strips, too. Match the folds, smoothing the quilt and strips. Slide a small mat under one end of the quilt, align the ruler with the edge of the quilt, then trim the border strips even with the quilt edge.**

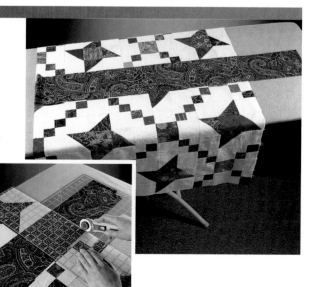

You can add border strips in any order, but for the most economical use of fabric, add the side ones first, before the top and bottom ones.

Fold the quilt in half to find the center of both side edges, then fold it in half again to find the quarter points. Mark the folds with pins as you did for the border strips.

Fold each side border strip in half to find the center of the long edge. Mark this point with a pin, or press a light crease in the fabric. Fold the strip in half again, and mark the quarter points.

Pin the border to the quilt top, matching the ends and the center and quarter marks.

If the border is slightly smaller than the quilt, or vice versa, you can ease in some fullness and make both edges fit by pinning them carefully. Pin the border to the quilt at 2-inch intervals, carefully easing in any excess fabric. Be sure to keep the quilt and the border aligned at the center and quarter marks.

Tip

Stitch with the fuller side against the feed dogs, letting the sewing machine do the work of easing the sides to fit.

Press the seam allowances toward the border whenever possible. Press along the seam first to set the stitches, then lift the border and press it gently into place. Be careful to avoid pressing pleats into the border strip when you press the border.

Avoid stretching the border by lifting it carefully, then setting the iron down on the seam. Do not pull the border toward the outer edge as you press. This will cause it to stretch and become distorted.

Tip

If you are using several borders, measure, trim, and sew each one separately for the best results.

8

Measure across the width of the quilt, through the center, including the attached borders. This gives you the length of the top and bottom border strips. Cut them 2 inches longer than the measurement. Fold the quilt if necessary, then trim the strips to fit the quilt as you did for the side borders. Determine the center and quarter measurements of both the borders and the quilt. Pin the borders to the quilt, easing as necessary, then sew them to the top and bottom edges.

Tip

If you are planning multiple borders for your quilt, square the corners after each border is added.

9

When all the border strips are attached to the quilt, make sure that the corners are really square. **Align a large acrylic ruler with the side edges of the quilt in one corner, then trim the corner if necessary.** Repeat with each corner.

Tip

Press the corner-square seams toward the border fabric so they'll be easy to match up when attaching the borders to your quilt.

10

To accommodate corner squares in a border, start by measuring, cutting, and trimming the border strips for the sides. For the top and bottom borders, measure the width of the quilt *without* the side borders. Sew the side borders to the quilt following Steps 5 and 6 on page 77. **From a contrasting fabric, cut four squares, each the dimension of the unfinished width of the borders. Stitch them to each end of the top and bottom borders.** Pin the borders to the quilt, matching the center marks, quarter marks, and the intersecting border seams, then stitch.

The Quilter's
Problem Solver

Border Bugaboos

Problem	Solution
It's challenging to choose colors for the border.	Try either a dark color or a bright one used in the quilt as a narrow (½ inch to 1 inch) inner border. This provides an accent at the edge of the quilt, leading your eye into the outer border. To create an illusion of depth in the borders, consider using two; use the lighter one as the inner border and the darker one as the outer border.
Seam lines in multiple borders are uneven.	After pressing the first border seam, straighten and trim the outer edge of the border. Measure, mark, and pin as with the first. When you stitch, sew with the quilt on top and try to keep the seam line parallel with the previously stitched one, even if it is wobbly. This way if your stitching wobbled slightly on the first seam, it will also on the second, and the narrow fabric border will appear straight.

Skill Builder

Some quilts can prove challenging when it is time to add the border.

If there is a discrepancy (more than 2 inches) between the actual length of the sides and the length of the middle of the quilt, take several measurements and use them to determine an average. If you must sew with the block edges underneath (rather than the border), be sure the block seams are firmly pressed, or even pinned, to avoid pushing them in the wrong direction as you sew the seam.

Try This!

To join border strips with a diagonal seam, place two strips right sides together at right angles. Overlap them by about ½ inch. Draw a line diagonally across the top strip from intersection to intersection, and sew on the line. Trim the seam allowance to ¼ inch; press the seam open. Match plaid and striped borders by cutting each strip from the same part of the fabric pattern. Fold the end of one strip at a 45 degree angle and move it along the adjacent strip until the patterns match.

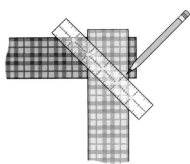

Perfectly
Mitered Borders

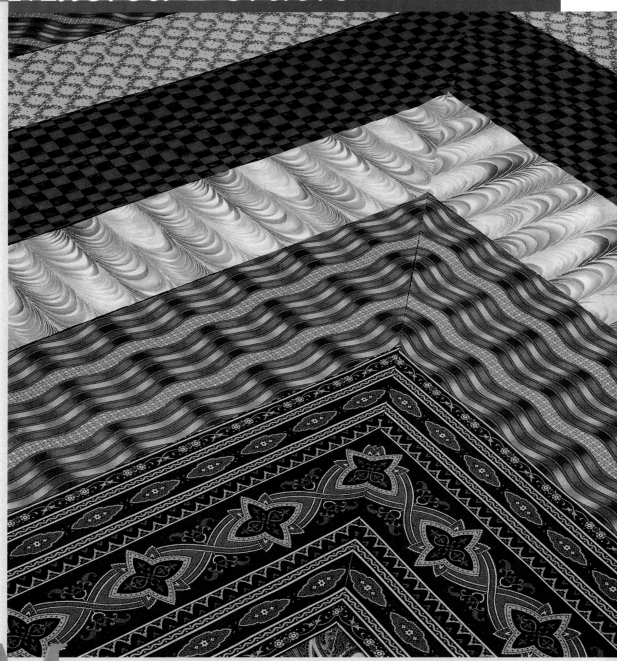

Mitering is considered to be the first-class way to finish the corners of the border, especially when the quilt contains diagonal designs and seam lines. It allows the two adjacent borders to meet gracefully at a 45 degree angle while they smoothly embrace the quilt and add to the radiating effect of the total design. Because mitering involves stitching angled seams along bias-cut edges, beginning quilters are sometimes afraid to attempt it. But have no fear, there are several easy ways to get perfectly mitered corners every time.

Getting Ready

When you're selecting border fabric, look for a printed border stripe that is compatible with the other fabrics in the quilt. There are many of these types of fabrics available today, and they make excellent borders, especially when you miter the corners. Most of the prints are symmetrical, making it easy to match the corners and sides. The prints can also form lovely secondary designs at the corners. Test your fabric selections by folding them lengthwise into a border-size strip and placing them at the edge of the quilt top.

There are several ways to miter corners. Read over the three methods described in "Mitering the Corners" on page 83, and choose the one that works best for you.

Read over the three methods described in "Mitering the Corners" on page 83

What You'll Need

Finished, pressed quilt top

Tape measure (a retractable metal one is best)

Border fabric

Rotary cutter and mat

6" × 24" rotary ruler with 45 degree line marked

45 degree triangle rotary ruler with ¼" markings (optional)

Pins

Chaco-liner rolling chalk wheel (optional)

Masking tape (optional)

Sewing machine

Thread

Thread snips

Iron and ironing board

Adding the Borders

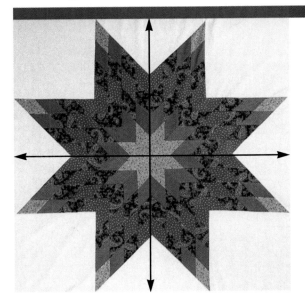

1

Measure the quilt top carefully, both its length and width. **The best place to measure a quilt is through the center, both lengthwise and crosswise. If you have a long seam in the middle of the quilt, measure along it for the best accuracy.** Edge measurements may be different from the center one, especially if the edges have stretched with handling. Your block sizes may also differ slightly from the planned ones, altering the expected measurements. By making the side or top and bottom edges the same length as the center, your quilt will hang or lie straight.

Tip

A metal tape measure is long enough to measure a whole quilt and will not stretch like cloth ones do.

2

Determine the best width for your border. A width that is a multiple of the block size is the most visually balanced. If you use several borders, make them different widths; this avoids a repetitive, stagnant look. The total border width should be no larger than the size of the block. **Cut border strips so they equal the length of the quilt, plus two times the width of the border, plus 2 to 3 inches for stitching.** For multiple borders, calculate the length of each one separately, or see "Try This" on page 85.

3

Find the center of the side border strips by folding them in half, and mark the centers with a pin. Unfold the border. **Starting in the center, measure half the length of the quilt along the border. Mark it with another pin. Measure and mark the other half in the same manner.** The ends of the quilt will be pinned to these marks. Refold the border strip, then fold it again, **bringing the center pin to meet the pins at the ends; pin each layer at the double fold.** This divides the border into quarters. There will be excess fabric at each end of the border. This is the overlap that will form the miter. Repeat these steps with the top and bottom borders.

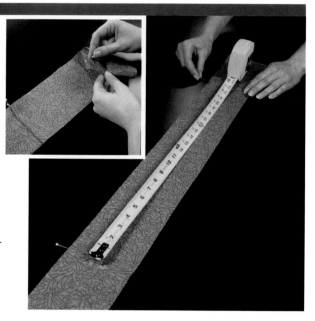

4

Fold the quilt top in half crosswise to find the center point of the sides, and fold it again to find the quarter points. **Place a pin at each of the divisions on each side.** Find the half and quarter divisions of the top and bottom edges in the same manner.

Pin the side borders to the quilt top, matching the half, quarter, and end marks. **Stitch them to the quilt, beginning and ending the stitching ¼ inch from each end.** Backstitch at each end. Pin and stitch the top and bottom borders in the same manner. Allow the excess border fabric to hang free.

Matching Striped Border Prints

To be effective, the designs on striped border prints must match at the corners. The key to a good match is to carefully cut the border strips. **For square quilts, cut all four borders so they are identical;** the printed designs should align all along the strips. **Align the center of the border with the center of the quilt edge, then miter the corners using the fold, press, and tape method (page 84).** The patterns will automatically match at each corner.

For rectangular quilts, cut identical strips for the top and bottom borders. Cut the side borders so the same part of the printed design that is on the ends of the top and bottom strips is at each end of these two strips. To adjust the fit of the side strips in the center, **fold the longer strips in half, matching the patterns on each end. Starting at the cut end, measure half the required border length and mark it.** Stitch across the strip, then trim the seam allowance to ¼ inch.

Tip

After you fold the longer borders in half, pin the matching patterns together.

Mitering the Corners

Pencil-and-Ruler Method

For the pencil-and-ruler method, fold the quilt diagonally so the right sides of adjacent borders are aligned and the raw edges match. **Lay a ruler along the fold and across the border edges, then draw a line from the end point of the border seam to the outer corner of the border.** Pin the seam, then stitch on the line, **beginning exactly in the corner where the borders join the quilt top.** Backstitch at the beginning, stitch along the drawn line, then backstitch at the end. Trim the seam allowances to ¼ inch.

Tip

For narrow (¼" to ⅜" wide) borders, it may be easiest to control the short mitered seams by stitching them by hand.

PERFECTLY MITERED BORDERS

1 Fold, Press, and Tape Method

The fold, press, and tape method keeps the bias edges aligned without pins. Arrange the corner on the ironing board with the right side of the quilt facing up. Overlap the border ends, making sure the corner is square. **Fold the top strip back until the edges of both border strips are aligned. Check the angle with a ruler, then press it. Center a piece of masking tape along the fold.**

2

Fold the quilt diagonally, draw a pencil line along the pressed line, then sew the corner. Stitch just outside the line to prevent catching the masking tape in the stitches. Trim the seam to ¼ inch.

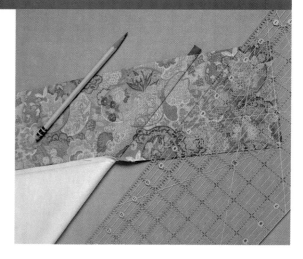

Pressing Tips

No matter which method you use, press the mitered seam open after stitching and trimming. This reduces the bulk and maintains the accuracy of the angle you have constructed. Press from the wrong side first to open the seam allowances, then press from the right side. Carefully smooth the corner into place, making sure that the borders are straight and the corners are flat. Press the border seams toward the border, making sure the corner of the quilt block covers the beginning of the miter. This will help the corner stay straight and flat.

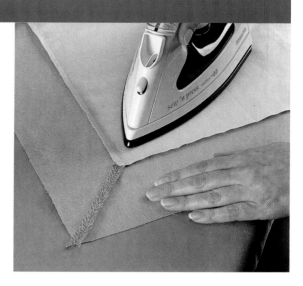

The Quilter's
Problem Solver

Less-Than-Perfect Mitered Corners

Problem	Solution
Corners of the border don't lie flat.	Check the angle of the miter. If it is slightly more than 45 degrees, the corner will ripple and not lie flat. If it is slightly less than 45 degrees, the corner will be too tight and will cup. Small discrepancies, less than ¼ inch, can usually be pressed or quilted out. Larger ones will need to be redone.
There are tiny holes or pleats at the beginning of the mitered seams.	Make certain the end points of adjacent border seams are lined up and the stitching begins at exactly the point where the two borders meet. If the two points are separated, the mitered seam will have a gap. If they are overlapped, the miter will begin with a small pleat. Pierce the seam intersections of both borders with a pin to align them. This may involve manipulating the border fabric a little, but it will ensure a perfect miter.

Skill Builder

The side borders of some quilts are designed to be narrower than the top and bottom ones, so the angle can't be 45 degrees.

You can still miter the corners of the border using the fold, press, and tape method. Lap the narrow border over the wide one (narrow one on top). Fold the narrow border back until its outer edge matches the outer edge of the wider border. Press the fold, then stitch on the fold line, either by hand from the right side or by machine from the wrong side.

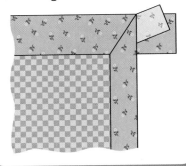

Try This!

If your quilt has several borders, you can stitch the strips together to form one wide border. Sew the borders to the quilt as usual, then miter the corners. It is much easier to handle the bulk of the quilt only once than it is to add each border separately. However, it is a little trickier to keep the mitering angle exact while you match each border strip to its mate. Hand stitching the mitered corner makes it easier to manipulate the borders so they match.

Fantastic Fit with
Pieced Borders

I f plain borders are the bread and butter in the world of quilts, pieced borders are the lavish desserts. A finely pieced, complex border is the ultimate achievement for a quilter who wants to test her skills. But not every pieced border has to be complicated—even a simple one adds a touch of class. With the tips and tricks that follow, you'll find lots of ways to design and fit a fantastic pieced border.

Getting Ready

While a plain border will complete your quilt quickly, a pieced border can enhance and transform it into a unique work. Choosing a design is the hardest part of making a pieced border. There are lots of ways to plan them and many things to consider. Look through books or magazines for pieced borders that appeal to you and that are compatible with your vision for the quilt. Study your quilt for motifs that might translate readily into a border. Determine which shapes are used most frequently and think about repeating them for the border design. Try dissecting the blocks into different parts that might work. To give you some ideas, here are a few examples of pieced border designs, ranging from simple to more complex.

 For information on measuring and adding borders, see "Simple Borders with Butted Corners" on page 74 and "Perfectly Mitered Borders" on page 80.

What You'll Need

Completed quilt blocks

Coordinating fabrics for borders

Rotary cutter and mat

6" × 24" rotary ruler

¼" or ⅛" graph paper and pencil

Tape measure (a retractable metal one is best)

Pins

Sewing machine

Thread

Thread snips

Iron and ironing board

Template plastic (optional)

Planning Pieced Borders

The border measurements determine the size of the motif and number of times you repeat it along the length of the border. **The easiest borders to plan and fit are those where the border unit, called the repeat, is the same size as the quilt block or the individual squares in the block.** Remember that the repeat size is a finished size; you must add seam allowances.

2

If you started planning your border with a specific repeat size in mind, you may find that the borders are not equally divisible by the proposed size. Try increasing or decreasing the size of the repeat by ¼ inch at a time until you find a size that fits both borders.

For example, if your quilt is 36 × 54 inches and the repeat is 4¾ inches, there are 11.36 repeats along the sides and 7.58 repeats on the top. But if you change the repeat to 3 inches, 18 will fit on the sides and 13 on the top and bottom.

Tip

To convert decimal figures to inches, remember that ¼" is 0.25 and ⅛" is 0.125 on the calculator.

3

Sometimes no number works equally for all sides. **The easiest solution is to add a narrow border before adding the pieced border.**

To calculate the cut width of the narrow side borders, measure the width of the quilt and the length of the top and bottom borders. Subtract the width measurement from the border length, then divide the result by 2. Add ½ inch for seams.

For the top and bottom borders, measure the length of the quilt, including the narrow border, and the length of the side borders. Subtract the quilt length from the length of the border, divide by 2, then add ½ inch.

Tip

These calculations determine only the border width. To calculate border length, see "Simple Borders with Butted Corners" on page 74.

4

Another way to make a pieced border fit is to design a pieced unit that relates to the border motif, perhaps a shortened or lengthened version of the repeat, to place in the center of the border.

For example, if one border is 1 inch too short or too long, you can either lengthen or shorten the size of the center repeat in that border to compensate. If the repeat is 4¾ inches, the lengthened unit would be 4¾ × 5¾ inches, or the shortened unit would be 4¾ × 3¾ inches.

Tip

If there are an even number of repeats in the incorrect border, adjust two repeats to maintain symmetry. Adapt each unit by half the difference.

Paper folding is the easy, no-math method used to figure out how many repeating units will fit and what size each of them should be. Cut a long strip of freezer paper or adding-machine paper to the exact size of the border, and fold it into equal sections. You may fold the paper in halves, quarters, and eighths, or you can fold it accordion-style, making sure the divisions are equal. **Use the smallest folded section as your measurement for the size of the finished repeat border unit.** Remember to add seam allowances to the finished measurement.

Tip

Make sure your folds are sharp and crisp to retain accuracy in the finished sections.

If you plan to use multiple pieced borders, the easiest way to make them all work together is to make sure that all the repeats are multiples of the same number. If the first border has 2-inch repeats, the second border should have 4- or 6-inch repeats to fit easily on the quilt. If you choose a plain border to go between the two pieced borders, make sure that it is also a multiple of your measurement. For a 2-inch repeat, a plain border could be 2, 4, or 6 inches wide.

Tip

Don't forget that you can also use half of the repeat measurement, especially if it is a plain border.

Deciding how to turn the corner of a pieced border is probably the most challenging part of designing. **If the border motif is a symmetrical square, such as the hourglass design, the piecing will turn the corner easily, continuing the design from one edge to the next. Pinwheel borders work in the same way.**

Some asymmetrical border designs, like Four Patch checkerboards, will turn the corner automatically if there are an uneven number of repeats on each side. Step 1 on page 96 of "Easy & Creative Pieced Borders" shows how this works.

Tip

If the border design is made of squares, a plain square is an easy way to turn the corner.

FANTASTIC FIT WITH PIECED BORDERS

Some directional designs, such as the Sawtooth, do not turn all four corners in the same way. **With directional patterns, a good solution is to change the direction of the repeats in the center of each border, making each half of the border the mirror image of the other half.** This allows all four sides and the corners to be identical. The motifs can simply reverse, or you can insert another design or a plain square in the center to ease the transition or to compensate for an odd number of blocks.

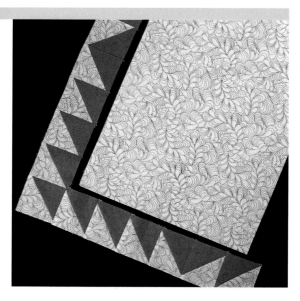

If your border design won't turn the corner easily, try a pieced corner block. Choose a block design that is related to the shapes used in the border, then draft it so it is the same size as the width of the borders. **Some simple pieced units, such as Square within a Square blocks, a triangle square, and many star designs, can also be used successfully to turn corners.**

A variation of the repeat that you can maneuver around the corner gives the border a more continuous look. **For example, you can adapt the tall triangle design to make a corner unit that turns nicely.**

Tip

A narrow inner border (½" to 1" wide) on a quilt acts like a mat on a picture, adding just a little accent.

Make sketches of the border design you have chosen, trying various options. Change the size of the elements or the frequency of the repeat, or try altering the number of borders you are planning. Pieced borders are often combined with plain borders, especially if you are having trouble getting a subsequent border to fit. Use the plain border as a spacer strip to make the quilt big enough to fit the border. See "Try This!" on the opposite page for details. Make a final quilt plan on graph paper, drawing the borders to scale.

The Quilter's
Problem Solver

Making Borders Fit

Problem	Solution
Border tends to stretch and grow because it has so many seams.	Make sure your cutting, sewing, and pressing are accurate. Handle the border carefully to avoid stress on the seams. Be sure that all pieces were cut with the outer edge on the straight grain. It is easier to keep the edges of the quilt straight if the outermost border is not pieced, so plan your quilts accordingly.
Pieced border is either too long or too short.	Prevention is easier than repair. Measure the border continually as you proceed with the stitching; if it becomes apparent that it is too long or too short, you can make adjustments in the piecing. Take slightly larger seams if the border is too big. If it is too small, make your seams a bit smaller than ¼ inch. This small difference is not usually noticeable.

Skill Builder

Don't press your pieced border until you have sewn it to the quilt.

By not pressing the pieced border before you sew it to the quilt, the border remains elastic and you can ease it more easily or fudge it to fit the quilt if necessary. If you press the strip, the elasticity is removed and it is more difficult to fudge it to fit. You must pin the border to the quilt very carefully, though, making sure that the seam allowances are pinned in the proper direction.

Try This!

You have completed your pieced border, only to discover that it is too long for the quilt, but the difference in length is not the same on both borders. There is no law that says that the border strips must be exactly the same size on both the top and bottom and the sides. You can add strips to the top and bottom edges that are slightly different from the ones you add to the sides to accommodate the piecing repeats exactly.

FANTASTIC FIT WITH PIECED BORDERS

Easy & Creative
Pieced Borders

E ven the most basic shapes make effective and interesting pieced borders. Contrasting light and dark squares can be arranged many different ways; they can be colored to look like flashing lights or a path of stepping stones. Flying Geese designs create a feeling of motion as they encircle a quilt. A combination of any of these designs can be a dramatic finale for any quilt.

Getting Ready

Measure the quilt top through the center both lengthwise and crosswise to determine the correct measurements for the borders. If the edges are a different measurement than the center, measure in several places. Average the numbers to determine your border length.

To determine the size and number of a design repeat in a border, start with a specific repeat size or a total number of repeats. Dividing the border measurement by the repeat size tells you the number of repeats. If the result includes a fraction, consider adding a spacer unit in the center of the border or changing the size of the repeat.

If you start with a specific number of repeats, divide the border measurement by that number to determine the size.

Four Patch Borders & More

For a Four Patch design to stand out, the blocks must be separated with spacers, otherwise the border will just look like a bunch of squares. **These spacers can be strips that are the same size as the individual patches, or they can be plain units the size of the Four Patch.** Use a third fabric for the spacer strips or blocks so the Four Patch units stand out.

You can also make the spacer unit from strips, using two of the fabrics in the Four Patch. **These units should be placed sideways to allow the darks and lights to alternate.**

Tip

To make all four corners identical, plan the piecing repeat so that there are an uneven number of Four Patches on each side of the quilt.

Tip

Always press
with the
straight grain
of the fabric to
help avoid
distortion.

2

To quick-piece simple Four Patch designs that require just two colors, cut a strip of each color across the width of the fabric. To determine the size of the cut strips, divide the finished repeat size by 2, then add ½ inch for seams.

Sew the strips together, matching the cut edges and stitching with an exact ¼-inch seam allowance. Press the seam toward the darker strip.

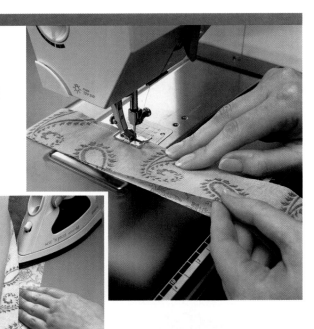

Tip

To make the
seams butt
more easily,
arrange cut
units so the
seam allow-
ance of the top
unit faces
toward the
needle as
you sew.

3

Cut segments from the pieced strip set the same width that you cut the individual strips. Arrange two segments with right sides together, making sure you reverse the color placement. Butt the seams, then sew the strips together. **You can chain stitch the four patch units to speed up the sewing and save thread.** If the patches are small and the fabric is firm, it may not be necessary to pin the patches together. Press the Four Patch units carefully, keeping the blocks square.

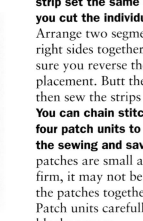

Tip

To determine
strip sizes,
divide the
repeat size by
three for Nine
Patch blocks
and five for Five
Patch blocks,
then add ½"
for seam
allowances.

4

You can easily adapt other blocks that are made with squares to use in borders. Nine Patch and Five Patch blocks are the most commonly used ones. You will need to arrange these units with spacer blocks or strips between them to retain the individual block designs. **Spacer units made from strips and placed sideways give an almost woven look to a Nine Patch or a Five Patch border.** Make sure that the colors alternate in the spacer strip.

Nine Patch blocks are easy to make with the same strip-piecing techniques you used for Four Patch blocks. Cut strips the required size (see the tip next to Step 4 on the opposite page). **Sew them together into two different sets of three strips each: one with dark on the outside edges, and one with light on the outside edges.** Cut the strip sets apart using the same measurement you used to cut the strips, then **sew the segments together, alternating the rows.**

Five Patch blocks are made the same way as Nine Patch blocks, but the strip sets are just a little different. You'll need to make two strip sets, each with five strips. **The first set has dark strips on the outer edges and in the center, while the second set has light strips on the outer edges and in the center.** To determine strip width, divide the repeat by five, then add ½ inch. Cut the strips, sew them together, and then cut them apart using the strip width measurement. **Arrange five segments, alternating the colors, then stitch them together to complete the block.**

Four, Five, or Nine Patch blocks set diagonally create even more interesting designs. To calculate sizes, choose your repeat size, making sure it fits both borders evenly. Multiply the repeat size by 0.707 to find the finished size of the block that will be set diagonally. Divide that by the grid in your pieced block to find the finished size of the individual segments. For example, if the repeat size is 6 inches, the finished size of the block is 4¼ inches (6 × 0.707). If the square is made of four smaller squares, each of the smaller squares is 2⅛ inches finished.

Tip

When you calculate the size of the smaller squares, don't forget to add seam allowances.

EASY & CREATIVE PIECED BORDERS

Tip

When sewing a bias edge to a straight edge, always sew with the bias on the bottom.

8

To join the blocks into a border strip, you will need to add side-setting triangles. To cut the triangles, multiply the finished size of the block by 1.414. Add 1¼ inches to the measurement, cut squares that size, then cut them along both diagonals. **Stitch the resulting triangles on two opposite sides of the squares, then sew the units together in a strip for the border.**

To make the triangles that form the corners at the ends of each strip, multiply the block size by 0.707 and add ⅞ inch to the measurement. Cut squares that size, then cut them along one diagonal.

Checkerboard Borders

1

Checkerboard designs form when blocks of alternating light and dark squares are placed next to each other with no spacer units between them. **The checkerboards occur automatically with blocks made of four squares.** Strip piecing makes them easy to construct, and they are fun to add to a quilt, either in just two colors, or made from a variety of different fabrics.

Tip

As long as you use an uneven number of piecing repeats on each side of the quilt, the checkerboard corners will be identical.

2

To accomplish the same checkerboard effect with Nine Patch or Five Patch blocks, you must make two different blocks and place them side by side. Alternate the placement of the dark and light squares so that one kind of block has dark corners and the other has light corners. When you place them together in the border, adjacent blocks will have opposite colors in the corners, continuing the checkerboard.

Flying Geese Borders

The Flying Geese pattern is based on a rectangle that is constructed with a large triangle and two smaller triangles. The large triangle is the "goose" and the smaller triangles are the background. **Traditionally, the ratio of length to width of a Flying Geese motif is 2:1. That is, it's twice as long as it is high.**

Try several different-size geese to determine the best size for your quilt. A row of large units might be the best choice, or perhaps two or more smaller rows separated by spacer strips would work better.

The easiest way to make Flying Geese is the "folded corner" method. **From the goose fabric, cut a rectangle the desired finished size plus ½ inch on both length and width.** From the background fabric, cut two squares, each half the width of the finished goose, plus ½ inch for seam allowances. For example, for a 2 × 4-inch finished goose, cut the rectangle 2½ × 4½ inches. Cut the background squares each 2½ × 2½ inches.

Draw a diagonal line on the wrong side of both background squares. **Place the first square on one corner of the goose rectangle with the diagonal line intersecting one corner.** Sew on the drawn line, then trim the seam allowance to ¼ inch. **Press the triangle toward the corner.** Repeat the procedure on the adjacent corner.

Always sew, trim, and press the first corner before constructing the second corner, because the squares overlap in the center.

Tip

Pay attention to the direction of the seam on the second square. You might end up with a parallelogram instead of a Flying Geese unit.

EASY & CREATIVE PIECED BORDERS

4

There are several ways to turn the corner of a Flying Geese border. Butted borders and plain corner squares are the easiest methods. **If you butt the corners, the Geese fill each border completely, but the turn is very abrupt and doesn't flow well. A plain square is the easiest way to turn the corner and provides an easy stopping and starting place for the design at each side of the quilt.**

5

Turning the corner with a pieced block gives the quilt extra pizzazz and is more graceful. The Square within a Square block shown is simple to construct and maintains the design elements of the border.

To construct this block, cut a square of goose fabric the same size as the width of the geese. Cut four squares of background the same size as the squares you cut for the geese. **Stitch a folded corner on two opposite corners of the square. Trim and press them, then add folded corners to the two remaining corners.**

6

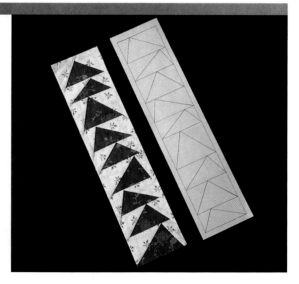

Tip

If your border is too long for one foundation strip, make several shorter segments and sew them together after they're pieced.

For a more whimsical Flying Geese design, make free-form or off-center geese using foundation piecing. Cut a piece of tracing paper the size of your border, including seam allowances. Mark the seam allowances on all four sides. **Draw the horizontal dividing lines, varying their distance from each other, then add diagonal lines to form triangles, varying the angles and the shape of the triangles.**

Begin piecing with the goose triangle on the bottom. Add the background triangles, then proceed with the next goose.

The Quilter's
Problem Solver

Fudging to Fit

Problem	Solution
In spite of careful measurements and accurate sewing, border is too long for the side of the quilt.	Try taking slightly deeper seams between repeats. If the border difference is not too great (no more than about 2 inches) the deeper seams won't show. This works especially well for borders made with squares, since the slight difference in the width of the squares is hardly noticeable.
Border is too short for the quilt.	You can unsew the seams between repeats and restitch them with a slightly smaller seam allowance if the discrepancy is 2 inches or less. This small difference in seam allowances is hard to see in the overall picture. You may not need to let out every seam. If this is so, space out your adjustments over the length of the border.
Border is more than 2 inches longer than the quilt.	Consider adding a narrow (1-inch-wide) border around the quilt to increase its size. In this case, you make the quilt fit the border rather than making the border fit the quilt.

Skill Builder

If the background fabric you are using for the Flying Geese is directional and you want the print to run in the same direction on each side of the goose, here's how to rotary cut the pieces.

Cut half the squares along one diagonal from the upper left to the lower right, and the other half on the opposite diagonal from the upper right to the lower left. Use one triangle from each group of squares on each side of the large triangle.

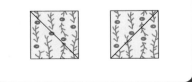

Try This!

You don't have to draw your quilt over and over to see what different borders might look like. Instead, sketch your quilt plan on graph paper, then place a piece of tracing paper over your drawing and sketch your border ideas on the tracing paper. You can try several different options without redrawing the quilt plan each time. When you have found the best border for your quilt, draw your final design, including the border, to scale on graph paper.

EASY & CREATIVE PIECED BORDERS

Quick & Easy
Strippy Borders

S trippy borders can be a quilter's best friend because they are both versatile and easy to make. They are great solutions for quilts that are made from strips, such as Log Cabins and Rail Fences. They neatly wrap up scrappy quilts, and they are fun to make with strips left over from your quilt. If these borders aren't already in your repertoire, now is the time to add them. If you've made strippy borders before, read on to find some fresh creative inspiration.

Getting Ready

Strippy borders often lie between two plain borders for stability, so when you plan your borders, plan for three—two plain and one pieced. Remember to keep the total border width no wider than the blocks.

Gather all the leftover fabrics from the quilt. Choose additional fabrics that coordinate with those in the quilt if desired, then cut strips from all the fabrics. Depending on the style border you choose, cut them all the same width or cut them in random widths from 1 inch minimum to 2¼ inches maximum. Cut strips at least 20 inches long. When you piece them together, the resulting strip set is wide enough to cut several border strips. You'll need about 32 to 40 strips for a twin-size quilt, and about 45 to 60 for a queen-size quilt.

 For information on measuring and adding borders, see "Simple Borders with Butted Corners" on page 74 and "Perfectly Mitered Borders" on page 80.

What You'll Need

Fabrics for border

Pencil

Rotary cutter and mat

6" × 24" rotary ruler

Pins

Sewing machine

Thread

Thread snips

Strippy Borders

A random-width strippy border is the easiest to piece, since there is no specific repeat measurement. Select a variety of strips 1 inch to 2¼ inches wide. Sew them together in groups of 8 to 10 strips. Press the seams all in the same direction, pressing carefully so the strip sets are flat. **Align a horizontal line on the ruler with one of the seams in the strip set, then trim away the uneven edge. Cut segments the width of your planned border, plus ½ inch for seam allowances. Sew segments together until the border is long enough for your quilt.**

Tip

Make sure the strip on each end of each border is a wider one. Very narrow strips don't give you leeway for trimming borders to fit.

2

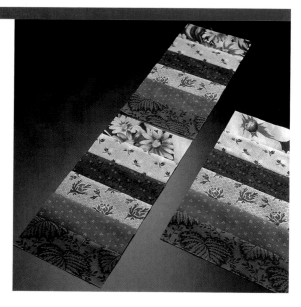

Cutting all the strips the same width is a slightly more formal treatment of a strippy border. **This works especially well when the fabrics are repeated in a regular pattern.**

To determine a repeat width for the strips, divide the quilt length and width by the proposed strip width. The result must be a whole number. For a quilt that is 27 inches by 36 inches, 1-inch- and 1½-inch-wide strips would both work, but 2-inch-wide strips would not. Follow the construction directions in Step 1 on page 101, making all the strip sets identical, with the same fabrics in the same order.

3

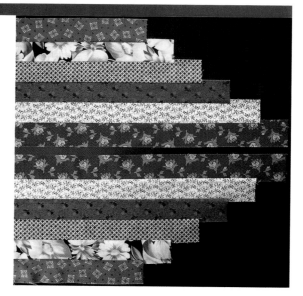

Tip

Add plain borders on both sides of a diagonal strippy border to stabilize the bias edges.

A diagonal strippy border is another interesting variation. Cut the strip sets at a 45 degree angle and reverse their direction in the center of the border for the easiest construction. You will need to cut a triangle to fill in the center space.

When you sew the strips together for the strip set, offset them by their width along the top edge for the most efficient use of fabric. Because you will be cutting angled segments in two directions, **make half the strip sets with the top angled in one direction and the other half with the top angled in the opposite direction.**

4

To trim the edge of the strip set, align the 45 degree line on your ruler with one of the seams in the strip set. Cut close to the edge. Cut segments your desired width, parallel to the first cut. Measure the length of the first segment along the top edge, then divide each border length by that measurement to determine how many segments to cut. Add about 2 inches extra to miter the corners.

To cut a triangle for the center of the border, cut a square 1¼ inches larger than the width of the segment, and cut it in half diagonally.

5

Arrange the segments on each side of the center triangle, then sew them together to form the border. Because the ends of the segments are cut at an angle, you will need to offset the segments by ¼ inch when you sew them together.

Before you add the border to the quilt, staystitch ⅛ inch from the two long edges to help stabilize it and make it easier to sew to the quilt. Be careful not to stretch the border while you are stitching.

Tip

Paper foundation piecing is a good alternative to strip piecing diagonal strippy borders. Start piecing in the center and work toward the ends.

6

Crazy piecing can make a great border. A low-contrast combination of fabrics adds interest to a quilt without overpowering it. Paper foundation piecing is the best way to construct a crazy-pieced border. Cut a piece of freezer paper the unfinished length and width of your border. **For easiest piecing, start in the middle of the border and work toward the ends.** Piece with strips or with other odd-size bits of fabric. Be sure to completely cover the paper foundation.

Tip

Try adding-machine paper for your foundation. It comes in widths up to 3⅞" wide and can be cut to the length of your border.

7

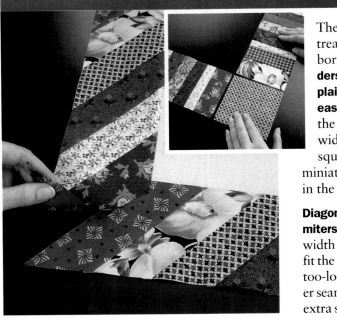

There are several options for treating the corners of strippy borders. **For straight strippy borders and crazy-pieced borders, plain corner squares are the easiest solution.** Cut the squares the same size as the cut border width. You can also add a pieced square in the corner, perhaps a miniaturized version of a block used in the quilt.

Diagonal strippy borders form natural miters. You may need to adjust the width of the strips to make the border fit the edge of the quilt exactly. Shorten too-long borders by taking slightly larger seams between each strip, and add extra strips if the border is too short.

QUICK & EASY STRIPPY BORDERS

103

Sawtooth &
Dogtooth Borders

Although there's an element of danger in their names, Sawtooth and Dogtooth borders have been quilters' friends for generations. Both classic border styles, based on triangles, are easy to accomplish with basic sewing skills. Either shape can be used alone as a border, but their simple elegance is multiplied when you combine them with plain or appliquéd borders, or when you use them in pairs. These are truly golden triangles; once you try them, you'll be delighted with the richness they add to your quilts.

Getting Ready

While Sawtooth and Dogtooth borders are both made with triangles, the Sawtooth border is always a right triangle (a square divided diagonally into two triangles). The Dogtooth border, on the other hand, can be made with many kinds of triangles, most commonly 60 and 90 degree triangles. Your choice may be determined by the graphic effect you desire, but if your border measurements do not divide into an even number of equal units, the Dogtooth may be the better choice, because the base and height of the triangle can be adjusted to fit the length and width of the border. Limit the fabrics to one or two of those in the quilt top, or choose a scrappy look with more variety. Just make sure there is plenty of contrast between the triangles and the background.

For information on measuring and adding borders, see "Simple Borders with Butted Corners" on page 74 and "Perfectly Mitered Borders" on page 80.

see "Simple Borders with Butted Corners" on page 74 and "Perfectly Mitered Borders" on page 80.

What You'll Need

- **Fabrics for border**
- **Waxed paper, tracing paper, *or* adding-machine paper**
- **Rotary cutter and mat**
- **Rotary ruler with 45 and 60 degree lines**
- **Pencil**
- **Pins**
- **Sewing machine**
- **Thread**
- **Thread snips**

Sawtooth Borders

For a Sawtooth border to turn all four corners the same way, the motif must reverse in the center of each side. There is an easy, nonmath way to determine the size of a repeat unit *and* to get it to reverse equally at the same time. **Cut a piece of paper half the length of the quilt and fold it to determine the size of the repeats.** Repeat for the quilt width. If you can't find a repeat measurement that fits both borders, first add a plain border to make the quilt fit the Sawtooth border.

Tip

Waxed paper, tracing paper, and adding-machine paper all work, but adding-machine paper is the easiest to use because it is the easiest to manipulate.

SAWTOOTH & DOGTOOTH BORDERS

2

To determine the total number of triangle squares needed to go around your quilt, count the number of folded segments on one strip of paper that is half the length of your quilt. Double that number to find the number of triangle squares to make for one side border, then double that number because you have two side borders. Repeat for the top and bottom borders.

Add the two numbers together, then add four more triangle squares (for the corners). This is the number of triangle squares you must make.

Tip

Since the Sawtooth border repeat is a square, the width of the border is determined by the size of the repeat.

3

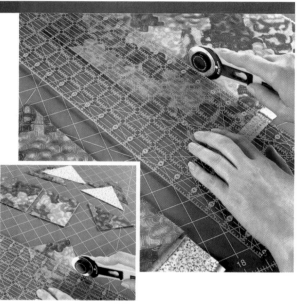

There are many ways to make triangle squares, but the easiest and most straightforward method is to cut squares, cut them once diagonally, and then sew two contrasting triangles together. To speed up the process, layer the background and triangle fabrics right sides together. **Fold the layered fabrics in half, then cut strips ⅞ inch larger than your finished triangle measurement.** Unfold the strips, keeping the triangle and background fabrics layered. Crosscut the layered strips into squares.

Without separating the layers, cut the squares diagonally, so the two fabrics are cut into triangles and ready to sew together.

Tip

Chain-piece the triangle squares together to save time and thread, being careful to keep them turned in the proper direction for your border.

Dogtooth Borders

1

The triangles in Dogtooth borders can be any angle, from very narrow to very wide.

For a 90 degree triangle Dogtooth border, cut squares that are 1¼ inches larger than the finished repeat size. Cut each square diagonally twice for four triangles. **Arrange them with their long sides along the long edges of the border, alternating the colors. Stitch the triangles together along their short sides, offsetting them by ¼ inch when you sew them together.**

Tip

These triangles don't need to reverse in the center, making it easier to plan the repeats.

A 60 degree Dogtooth border is another attractive option. The repeat measurement is the finished size of the base of the triangle. To determine the cut width of the strip, draw the finished triangle on a piece of graph paper. Measure the height of the triangle, and add ¾ inch. Cut strips of triangle and background fabric that width. **Align the 60 degree angle of the ruler along the bottom of the strip, and cut. Turn the ruler around so the 60 degree angle is at the top of the strip, and finish cutting the triangle.** Repeat along the strip.

Tip

If you have a 60 degree triangle rotary ruler, this is a good place to use it.

For the easiest way to construct a 60 degree Dogtooth border, layer the triangle and background fabrics right sides together before you cut the strips. Keep them layered as you cut the triangles. **Sew the pairs of triangles together along one of the bias edges.** Press the seams toward the darker fabric.

Arrange pressed units with right sides together and the colors alternating. **Offset the ends by ¼ inch, and sew them together.**

You are not limited to 45 degree and 60 degree triangles for Dogtooth borders. Try very long, skinny triangles or shorter, fatter ones. To draft them, cut a piece of paper the finished width and length of the border and fold it to determine the repeat measurement. Fold one segment in half lengthwise to find its center, and make a mark at the fold line. **Draw lines from each corner of the base to the center mark on the top of the segment.** Make a template from your drafted triangle to cut the pieces for the border.

Tip

You can also use the template to draft a pattern for foundation piecing, as described on page 108.

SAWTOOTH & DOGTOOTH BORDERS

5

A Dogtooth border is sometimes easier to appliqué than to piece. Cut a strip of triangle fabric that is ½ inch wider than the finished Dogtooth triangles and as long as the required border. Baste it to the edge of a strip of background fabric cut the width and length of the border, including seam allowances. Make a template following the directions in Step 4 on page 107, and mark the pattern on the triangle fabric. Do not cut the entire pattern. **Cut only one to two triangles ahead of your stitching to avoid stretching and fraying the border.**

6

There are several ways to turn the corner of a Dogtooth border. **The easiest treatments are either plain squares made of the triangle fabric or triangle squares in the corners.** Assemble the quilt as you did for borders with cornerstones (Step 7 on page 39).

The other option is to design a corner square with a variation of the Dogtooth triangle. You can place the apex of the triangle on the inside corner or the outside corner of the border.

Foundation-Pieced Borders

All of these borders are very easy to construct using a paper foundation. The borders will be extremely accurate because the paper is cut to the exact required size, and it doesn't stretch like pieced borders sometimes do.

Draw your border on tracing paper or another foundation paper. Adding-machine paper, if it is wide enough, is ideal for foundations. To save fabric and make the piecing a little easier, make a template the size of the triangle plus ½-inch seam allowances. **Use it to cut oversize triangles from the triangle and background fabrics for the foundation piecing.**

Tip

If the foundation is too long and gets in the way, roll up one end and secure it with a paper clip.

The Quilter's
Problem Solver

The Trouble with Triangles

Problem	Solution
Triangle tips got cut off during binding.	When you bind the edge of a Sawtooth border, you have to stitch across the triangles blind. It is easier to get nice, sharp triangle tips if you add a plain border before you bind the quilt. When you stitch the border in place with the triangle border on top, it is easy to keep the tips accurate.
Edge of the border is very stretchy.	Cut all the triangles with their base along the straight grain. This will help stabilize stretchy edges. To fix the stretchy border, run a line of staystitching ⅛ inch from the edge of the border. Be careful not to stretch the edge as you stitch. If there is a lot of stretch, stitch a line of basting along the edge, then pull up the thread until the border is the correct length. Spread the fullness evenly along the border, then staystitch the edge.

Skill Builder

Multiple rows of Sawtooth triangles provide a dramatic border for your quilt.

Appliqué blocks in particular, especially those with a lot of background space showing and very simple appliqués, can benefit from the addition of several rows of Sawtooth borders. Use several shades of the same color in the borders so they don't become too repetitive.

You can even use the Sawtooth triangles as sashing strips between blocks to increase the drama. Add a wide (6 inches or more) plain border after the Sawtooth ones to balance the center design.

Try This!

Add pizzazz to your 60 degree Dogtooth borders by making multicolor triangles.

Cut strips of two different triangle fabrics, each half the cut width of the background strip, plus ¼ inch for seam allowances. Sew them together, then layer this new strip with a strip of background fabric. Cut your 60 degree triangles as usual. Half the triangles will have one color at the base, the remaining triangles will have the second color at the base.

Painless
Borders

Not all borders are added after the fact. If you set the blocks of your quilt on the diagonal and use specially designed blocks at both ends of each row, you can make a quilt that sports a pieced border without having to do complex math or intricate sewing. These are called painless or integrated borders because the border is contained in these special quilt blocks, rather than created by piecing a separate border. The math and piecing are truly almost painless. In this lesson we show you how to make the blocks for two integrated border variations—a Big and Little Squares border and a Sawtooth border.

Getting Ready

Gather your quilt blocks, but don't sew them together yet. (Unfortunately, these borders do not work on quilts that are already set together). Before you sew any blocks together, you must construct the border and corner blocks. And since these quilts are set diagonally, you must also cut side-setting and corner triangles.

Sketch your quilt design on graph paper. Draw squares the same size as the design blocks for the border blocks. Count the number of side border blocks and corner blocks (always four) required for your quilt.

Big & Little Squares Border

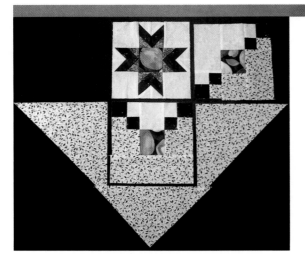

A quilt with a painless border is made of several parts, all of which are included in the blocks. The *background* is the fabric used as the background of the design blocks, in this case, the white print. The *pieced border* includes either the squares or triangles placed next to the background that outline the interior designs. The *outer border* is usually a print fabric that lies between the pieced border and the outer edge.

Tip

If your block measurement is not easily divisible by 3, read about the Sawtooth border on page 105. It may work better.

Referring to the block designs in the photo, draw the border and corner block designs on your graph paper sketch. These border blocks are based on a Nine Patch grid, so they work best with blocks that are easily divisible by 3, such as 6-, 7½-, 9-, 10½-, or 12-inch blocks.

3

Tip

You might want to paste swatches of the appropriate fabrics in each square to test the contrast.

Choose fabrics for the pieced border and the outer border. A print fabric works best for the outer border because it disguises the seams between the blocks. For the pieced border, try to repeat some of the colors used in the blocks. You can use anywhere from one to five fabrics for the pieced border. The one shown here requires two different blue prints.

Be sure there is enough contrast between the pieced border and the outer border and between the pieced border and the background.

4

Measure your quilt blocks to determine the finished size (actual size less ½ inch for seam allowances). To determine the measurement of all the pieces for the border blocks, divide the measurement by three. This is the finished size of each large square in the border block. The small square is half this measurement. In the example shown, the finished block is 7½ inches; therefore, the large squares will be 2½ inches finished (7½ ÷ 3) and the small squares will be 1¼ inches finished (2½ ÷ 2). Be sure to add ½ inch to the squares for seam allowances.

PAINLESS BORDERS

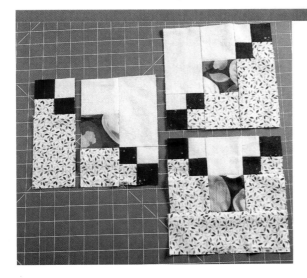

Cut squares of background, border, and outer border fabric to the correct size. If you cut strips of fabric across the width, you can then crosscut the appropriate squares more easily. Strip piece the smaller Four Patch squares. **Cut strips of background and border square fabric the same size as the smaller squares, then sew them together to make a strip set.** Do the same thing with the outer border and border square fabric. Cut them into segments that are the same width as each cut strip.

Assemble the smaller Four Patch units for the corners of each block, then **sew the remaining pieces together to complete the side border blocks and the corner blocks.** Make as many side border blocks as you need for your quilt. You will always need four corner blocks.

Tip

Make sure the Four Patch units are oriented properly. It's easy to turn them around.

On a design wall or on the floor, **arrange the blocks for the body of the quilt, then add the side border blocks and corner blocks around the outer edges.** Add the side-setting triangles and corner triangles last. (Refer to Steps 4 and 5 on pages 32 and 33 for determining cutting dimensions.) Check to be sure that all the blocks are oriented in the proper direction, especially the border blocks.

Pick up the blocks in diagonal rows, and sew them together, being sure to stitch a side-setting or corner triangle at each end. Sew the rows together.

PAINLESS BORDERS

113

Sawtooth Border

1

You can adapt these techniques to make a Sawtooth border, too. **The blocks are constructed with squares and triangle squares.** This border works best with blocks that are an even size—6, 8, 10, or 12 inches, for example. Divide the finished block size by four to determine the finished size of the small squares and half-square triangles needed for the border blocks. Divide the finished block size by two to determine the finished size of the larger squares.

2

Make a paste-up block as you did for the Big and Little Squares border. Check the contrast between the fabric for the triangles and the background and border fabrics.

Make triangle squares the desired size (don't forget to add ⅞-inch seam allowances). Then cut squares of both background and outer border fabric as required, remembering to add ½ inch for seam allowances.

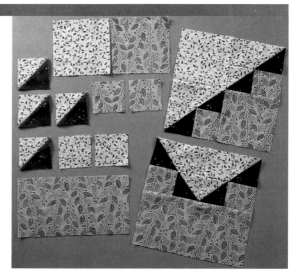

3

Arrange the squares in the proper order, then sew them together to create the outer border and corner blocks. Arrange the blocks with the side-setting and corner triangles, and sew them together as you did in Step 7 on page 113 for the Big and Little Squares border.

Tip

Check the orientation of the border blocks before you sew them together. It's easy to get one block oriented in the wrong direction.

The Quilter's
Problem Solver

Playing with Color

Problem	Solution
Lots of colors in the blocks. Can the borders help tie them all together?	When you make Four Patch units for the border blocks, use a variety of colors for the border squares. Use short strips of a variety of colors to make the strip sets described in Step 2 on page 94. Construct triangle squares with several of the colors used in the main body of the quilt. Vary their placement in the border and corner blocks.
Pieced border doesn't show up very well.	Contrast between the outer border, the background, and the pieced border is essential. When you audition fabrics for the pieced border, arrange them so that representative amounts of each fabric are visible. Stand at least 6 to 8 feet back from the fabrics to be sure that the contrast is good. When in doubt, the background fabric almost always looks good as the outer border fabric, and there is usually plenty of contrast.

Bias edges, such as those found on the side-setting triangles, can become misshapen or misaligned.

When that happens, and you are trying to sew the rows together, it is hard to make the rows straight. For a sure-fire fit, try cutting the corner and side-setting triangles a bit larger than necessary. Make sure the edge of the side-setting triangle is even with the row of blocks. If it is not, either trim the triangle, or remove it and restitch so that it is even.

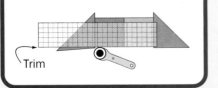

Trim

Try This!

These two tips will help you solve some of the problems associated with diagonally set quilts.

❏ The bias edges on the side-setting and corner triangles can stretch as you sew them. If you sew these units with the triangle on the top, the presser foot will make the bias edges stretch. Sew these units with the triangle on the bottom to minimize this stretching.

❏ To make it easier to sew rows together accurately, trim the tips of the triangles before you pin and sew the next row.

Trim →
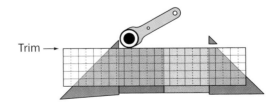

Planning
Appliquéd Borders

Don't overlook the touch of class that an appliqué border can add to your quilt, whether the quilt is pieced or appliquéd. Appliqué borders, while offering great style, also have other advantages. They are easier to fit, they are often faster to construct than pieced borders, (yes, really) and the curves of an appliqué design offer a beautiful counterpoint to the straight lines of a pieced pattern. Appliqué offers lots of marvelous creative options for your borders.

Getting Ready

An appliqué border design should be compatible with the style of the quilt. While the border motifs of an appliqué quilt are often limited to variations of those used in the blocks, a pieced center provides lots more options. Look through appliqué design books and select several ideas to preview. Use more primitive motifs with scrap designs or folk style or whimsical blocks. If your quilt design is more formal, choose formal appliqué motifs for the border. Just remember, the border needs to fit the mood of the quilt, whether it is a casual, primitive, or more elegant design.

Plan for the widest border that is compatible with your quilt design—an appliqué border is important, and it shouldn't be too narrow.

What You'll Need

- **Freezer, tracing, or waxed paper**
- **Pencil**
- **Fabric for border and appliqués**
- **Rotary cutter and mat**
- **6" × 24" rotary ruler**
- **Washable marking pencil**
- **Black marking pen**
- **Pins**
- **Sewing machine**
- **Thread**
- **Thread snips**
- **Iron and ironing board**
- **Spray starch (optional)**
- **Wash-A-Way water soluble basting thread (optional)**

Creating an Appliquéd Border

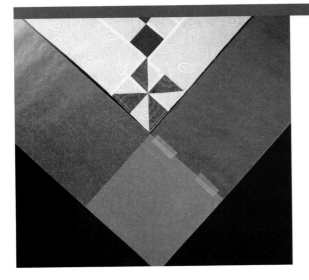

1

Cut two strips of freezer paper, tracing paper on a roll, or waxed paper. One should be half the length of the top plus the border width, the other should be half the length of the side plus the border width. Both should be the finished width of the border without seam allowances. **Tape the strips together to form a corner.** Use this basic pattern to play with the motifs and design your border. You can make a full-size pattern if you wish, but the half-size one will be enough to design your border motif and corner treatment.

Tip

Make two border patterns—one of waxed or tracing paper for a master pattern and the other of freezer paper to cut up for appliqué patterns.

2

Tip

If your design is asymmetrical, you will have to trace the entire border on the paper.

Measure the quilt, then choose a pattern with a repeat that fits the measurements. For example, if your quilt is 60 inches square, the repeat should be a multiple of 60, such as a 5, 6, or 10 inches. When the length and width of the quilt differ, the repeat should fit both. For a 45 × 60-inch quilt, a 5-inch repeat would work. **Fold your wax paper pattern accordion style to the size of the repeats. Trace the repeat unit of the design on the top layer of the folded waxed paper; when you unfold it, you can see the whole design.**

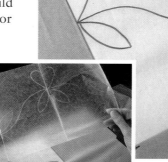

3

Tip

Plan ahead. How your appliqué turns the corner can determine whether borders with mitered or butted corners will work best.

There are several ways to carry a design around a corner. **Make a vine turn gracefully by having two vine ends from adjacent borders curve and meet in the corner.** Cover the intersection with a floral or leaf motif.

Adapt the design repeat for the corner. Fold a square of waxed paper diagonally. Place the center of the motif on the fold, then trace it. Unfold the waxed paper to see the result. A mitered corner works well for this kind of treatment. **Sometimes a separate compatible motif is the best corner solution.** Borders with corner squares work best for this kind of design.

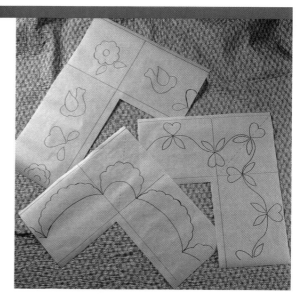

4

Tip

A light box will make the job of tracing the pattern a little easier.

When you have determined your corner style, cut the fabric for the borders. (Refer to pages 74 and 80 for directions for measuring and cutting butted and mitered borders.) Add about 2 inches to the length of each border in case the appliqué shrinks the border. Lightly mark the seam allowances on all sides of each border.

Trace over the lines on your master pattern with a black marking pen so the design shows through the fabric. **Transfer your appliqué pattern onto the border as a placement guide.** Draw it lightly on the border, or see "Skill Builder" on page 121 for some other marking options.

Appliqué the borders. **If you have chosen a design that goes around a corner, appliqué to about 2 inches from the seam, leaving the remainder of the appliqué unfinished.** You will complete it after the borders are added to the quilt. Press the borders carefully. Check the fit of the borders, making sure the seam marks align ¼ inch from the quilt edge. Repeat for all borders and stitch them to the quilt. Be sure to keep the loose pieces of any continuous appliqué pinned out of the way as you attach the borders.

Pad the ironing board with a terry cloth towel, and press from the wrong side to avoid flattening the appliqué.

6

If the appliqué has made the border shrink slightly, you will need to adjust the appliqué pieces at the corner. **Arrange any vines or other motifs so that they turn the corner gracefully.** Make sure that the seams are covered or carefully stitched at the intersection of the continuous motif. Complete the appliqué that was left unfinished, then carefully press it.

Design Ideas

Pieced Border Accent

A pieced border makes a lovely bridge between an appliquéd quilt center and an appliquéd border. On many old appliqué quilts, the outer border is separated from the inner design with a row of triangle squares that form a Sawtooth border. The contrast of the angular Sawtooth with the curved appliqué emphasizes both the border and the inner design.

A geometric appliquéd border, such as the Dogtooth described on page 104, can also effectively frame an appliqué border.

PLANNING APPLIQUÉD BORDERS

Appliqué on a Pieced Background

Tip

Machine
appliqué makes
it easy to deal
with the
multiple layers
of fabric in
pieced borders.

Try appliquéing motifs on a pieced border for another alternative. Be sure that there is enough contrast between the background piecing and the appliqué motifs. With low contrast, the appliqué shapes will tend to disappear on the pieced border. **Crazy pieced, strip pieced, or simple geometric shapes in subtle colors are a good choice for the background of the appliqué.** Try a collection of background-style prints in one color family. Folk style quilts can benefit especially from the addition of appliqué on piecing.

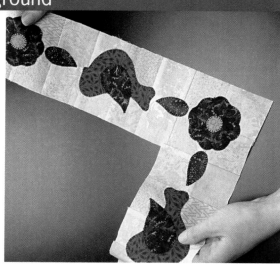

Appliqué on Sides

Tip

Use the
appliqué design
for a quilting
pattern on the
rest of the
border to
effectively
accent both
elements.

An appliqué border doesn't have to turn the corner at all. It can extend along the edges from the center and not quite meet in the corners. **Try a distinctive motif in the center of each side with other elements extending toward the corners.** This works very well on quilts that are longer in one dimension than the other because you can easily adjust the motifs to fit both border lengths.

You can also appliqué motifs in just two opposite corners, leaving the two remaining corners plain. Bows and ribbons are particularly effective motifs for this kind of border.

Appliquéing Irregular Edges

Tip

To mark the
turn-under line,
stitch ¼" from
the edge of the
quilt top with
Wash-A-Way
water soluble
basting thread.

If you dread the chore of binding a quilt with an irregular edge, think appliqué! **Appliqué the troublesome edge to a border strip.** This is a great way to deal with patterns such as Grandmother's Flower Garden and Double Wedding Ring, where the edges follow the shapes of the hexagons, circles, or diamonds. The border not only accents the shaped edge of the quilt top, but also makes binding much easier.

The Quilter's
Problem Solver

Freezer Paper Appliqué

Problem	Solution
Cutting the backing away to retrieve freezer paper templates makes the quilt less stable.	Press the freezer paper to the right side of the fabric. The paper edge serves as a turn-under guide, and the freezer paper is easy to remove from the top side. Or try cutting your pattern shapes from clear Con-Tact paper. Stick them on the right side of the fabric. The Con-Tact paper will adhere until it is removed, it does not leave a residue on most fabrics, and the edge is firm enough for a needle-turning guide. Remove it before pressing, though—heat melts the plastic!
Freezer paper falls off the appliqué fabric pieces.	When you press the paper onto the fabric, press on a hard surface, such as a breadboard. Heat the iron to the wool setting, and leave it in place as you count to 10.

Skill Builder

Here are two no-mark alternatives if you prefer not to draw the appliqué placement on the border. This way you can change your mind about the design, and you don't have to worry about whether the appliqué patches cover the marks.

❏ Pin your waxed or tracing paper master pattern to the border. Slip the appliqué pieces under the paper to position them.

❏ Tape your master pattern to a light table, lay the border on top, and position the pieces. The dark lines on your master pattern will show through even darker fabrics.

Try This!

Design ideas for appliqué borders can come from many sources.

❏ If you have used a larger-scale fabric in your quilt, see if it contains motifs that might be cut out and appliquéd to the border. Flowers or birds are particularly useful for this purpose.

❏ Check smaller prints for designs that can be enlarged and used on the border.

❏ Consider shading the border appliqué, making it progressively lighter or darker as it goes around the quilt.

Sets & Borders
Glossary

A

Alternate block. A plain, pieced, or appliquéd block used to separate the basic blocks in the quilt.

Appliqué. Sewing small pieces of fabric, by hand or by machine, onto a larger background.

B

Bar set. A linear setting created when blocks are sewn together in horizontal or vertical rows, with rows separated by sashing.

Basic block. The primary block, or starting point, for the quilt. It can be pieced or appliquéd, or both.

Between blocks. Blocks in a diagonal set that fill in the spaces between the basic blocks. These might be made from an alternate block, or they might be the same as the basic blocks.

Bias. The stretchy, diagonal grain of the fabric. True bias is at a 45 degree angle to the straight grain, but any off-grain cut may be referred to as a bias cut.

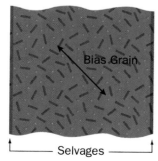

Bias Grain

Selvages

Blocking. Manipulating an irregular block while pressing in order to make it the exact size and shape it should be.

Border print. A fabric with a series of one or more decorative stripes, each printed lengthwise on the cloth. Border prints often work best when used with mitered borders. See *Mitered borders.*

Borders. Plain, pieced, or appliquéd strips of fabric sewn around the outer perimeter of a quilt top. Borders act as a frame for the inner body of the quilt.

Butted borders. Borders sewn along the entire length or width of the quilt, including the ends of previously added borders. Border seams are parallel to the quilt sides. Also called straight or overlapped borders.

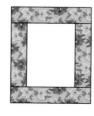

C

Chain piecing. An assembly line technique where pieces are paired together, then fed through the sewing machine one after another without lifting the presser foot or cutting the threads.

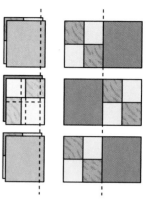

Corner triangle. A right triangle with the straight grain parallel to its short edges. Used to form the corners of a diagonally set quilt.

Cornerstone. A square sewn between sashing strips at the corners of each block or at corners where borders meet. Also referred to as corner blocks.

Crazy piecing. Sewing randomly sized and shaped patches of fabric to a foundation to form a border or a block. Also called crazy patch.

Crosswise grain. Fabric threads running perpendicular to the selvages, going across the fabric from side to side. Formed by weft threads, which were woven back and forth along the lengthwise grain during the weaving process.

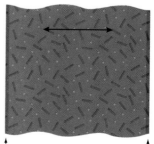

Selvages

D

Design wall. A permanent or portable design area covered with felt, flannel, or batting that allows blocks and other design elements to stick to its surface without pinning.

Diagonal set. A quilt layout where the sides of blocks are at a 45 degree angle to the sides of the quilt.

Directional print. Fabric printed with a design that flows in one direction, such as stripes.

Drafting. The process of designing a quilt block to fit a desired finished size.

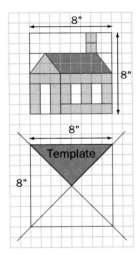

Drop. The portion of the quilt from the edge of the bed to the floor. It may extend all the way to the floor, or end at a point between the edge of the bed and the floor.

E

Easing. Manipulating and adjusting two uneven edges so that they match for sewing.

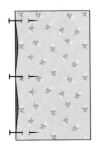

Equilateral triangle. A triangle with all three sides the same length and all three corners the same angle.

F

Finished size. The size of a patch or block after it has been sewn to all neighboring patches. Finished size does not include seam allowances.

Floating the blocks. Using oversize setting elements that blend with block components around the quilt perimeter. Block edges do not touch borders, which makes them appear to float.

Foundation. A temporary or permanent material used as a base on which to sew smaller pieces of fabric.

Freezer paper. A roll of paper that is plastic-coated on one side. Its original purpose was for freezing foods, but quilters have carried it off to the sewing room for foundation piecing, template making, and appliqué.

G

Geometric print. Fabric that is printed with a pattern of lines, squares, or other geometric shapes. Checks, plaids, and stripes are included in this category of fabrics.

Graph paper. Gridded paper that can be used as foundation material or to draft quilt blocks. It is also helpful in testing for a perfect ¼-inch seam allowance.

H

Hera. A traditional Japanese marking tool that leaves a sharp crease where it is pulled across fabric. The crease can be used to indicate stitching lines.

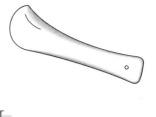

I

Inside blocks. See *Between blocks.*

Integrated borders. Border elements assembled into blocks. When blocks are joined, pieced borders are created automatically.

Ironing. Moving an iron back and forth across the surface of yardage to remove wrinkles to prepare it for cutting. See *Pressing.*

J

Jigsaw puzzle set. A quilt containing a variety of blocks or other pieced units, in assorted sizes, often left over from other projects. Units are assembled in much the same way as a jigsaw puzzle is, by determining which pieces fit best in each position.

L

Lattice. See *Sashing.*

Lengthwise grain. Fabric threads running parallel to the selvages. Formed by warp threads, which were attached to the loom during the weaving process. The less stretchy of the two straight grains.

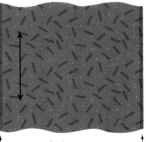

Selvages

Light box. A glass- or Plexiglas-topped box containing a bright light that makes tracing quilting patterns a breeze. Commercially made light boxes are available from quilt shops or art supply stores. You can make a temporary version by placing a light beneath any glass or Plexiglas table.

Medallion quilt. A setting with a strong central motif surrounded by a series of borders or other design elements.

Mirror image. Any image that is the exact opposite of an original image.

Mitered borders. Borders sewn together with a 45 degree seam at adjoining corners.

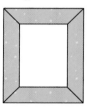

Multiview lens. A lens that reflects multiple images of the object being viewed. For instance, one quilt block appears to be many identical blocks positioned side by side.

Off-grain. A fabric that is printed so the pattern does not follow the straight grain, or a pattern piece that is not cut with the straight grain on at least one edge.

On point. See *Diagonal set.*

Orientation. The direction in which you point the edges of your quilt blocks—for example, straight or diagonal.

Orphan block. Unused block from a prior project.

Painless borders. See *Integrated borders.*

Pieced borders. Borders made up of smaller units pieced together to form a long strip, rather than one single piece of fabric.

Plain block. A block cut from a single piece of fabric, often used as an alternate block in quilt settings.

Pressing. Bringing the weight of an iron straight down on quilt pieces without moving the iron back and forth, in order to flatten seams without stretching or distorting the unit. See *Ironing.*

Quick-piecing. See *Strip piecing.*

Reducing lens. A lens that reduces the size of objects being viewed, making them appear farther away. Ideal for viewing block settings and gauging their overall effect.

Repeat. The unit in a border that is duplicated and stitched together, side by side, with other identical units to create the border.

Rotary cutter. A fabric cutting tool that resembles a pizza cutter, but with a razor-sharp blade capable of slicing through several layers of fabric at once.

Rotary-cutting ruler. Also referred to as a see-through or acrylic ruler, this thick, rigid ruler allows quilters to measure fabric strips and hold them in place securely for rotary cutting.

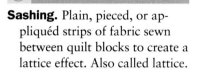

Sashing. Plain, pieced, or appliquéd strips of fabric sewn between quilt blocks to create a lattice effect. Also called lattice.

Sashing square. See *Cornerstone.*

Seam allowance. The fabric between a stitched seam and the raw edge of patches.

Secondary pattern. A pattern that forms when four blocks are arranged in a square. The new pattern is not obvious in the original block and is only visible when the blocks are arranged together.

Segment. A piece cut from a strip set.

Selvage. Tightly woven, finished edges that run lengthwise along the fabric. They should be trimmed away and not used.

Set or setting. The manner in which individual quilt components are arranged to form the overall design of a quilt top.

Setting square. A plain block used between basic blocks.

Side-by-side setting. Sewing blocks together with no other elements between them.

G L O S S A R Y

Side-setting triangle. A right triangle with the fabric's straight grain parallel to its longest edge. Used to fill in the gaps along the outer edges of a diagonally set quilt.

Staggered set. A layout where the orientation of blocks shifts from row to row. Sashing strips or other units are used as spacers for the shifts.

Straight grain. Threads that run parallel or perpendicular to the selvages in a bolt of fabric. See *Crosswise grain* and *Lengthwise grain.*

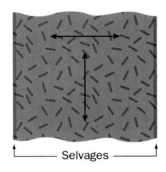

└ ── Selvages ── ┘

Straight set. An arrangement where the sides of the quilt blocks are parallel to the sides of the quilt.

Strip piecing. A quick-piecing technique where long strips of fabric are cut to specific widths and lengths, and then they're sewn together lengthwise into strip sets. Shorter segments are cut from each set, then sewn together to create a pieced unit.

Strippy piecing. A quick-piecing technique where random-width strips of fabric are sewn together, then shapes are cut from the resulting pieced cloth.

Strippy set. See *Bar set.*

Template. An exact copy of a pattern piece, used as a guide for marking, cutting, or positioning fabric.

Tracing paper. Lightweight see-through paper that is available in art supply or department stores. It comes in sheets or on a roll. When placed over a design in a book, the lines are easily visible and can be copied to the tracing paper, then transferred to fabric or template material.

Triangle square. A commonly used patchwork unit made up of two right triangles sewn together on their longest edge to form a square. Sometimes referred to as half-square triangle.

Waxed paper. A roll of see-through paper with a wax coating on both sides. It was originally made for wrapping food, but quilters have adopted (and adapted) it to use in designing borders. When you fold it into several layers and draw on the top layer, the markings are transferred to the layers underneath, providing a drawing of an entire border with less work.

Zigzag set. A set where on-point blocks are sewn into rows with setting triangles on each side, then rows are joined. Also called Streak of Lightning.

METRIC EQUIVALENCY CHART

mm=millimeters
cm=centimeters

Yards to Meters

YARDS	METERS	YARDS	METERS	YARDS	METERS	YARDS	METERS	YARDS	METERS
⅛	0.11	2⅛	1.94	4⅛	3.77	6⅛	5.60	8⅛	7.43
¼	0.23	2¼	2.06	4¼	3.89	6¼	5.72	8¼	7.54
⅜	0.34	2⅜	2.17	4⅜	4.00	6⅜	5.83	8⅜	7.66
½	0.46	2½	2.29	4½	4.11	6½	5.94	8½	7.77
⅝	0.57	2⅝	2.40	4⅝	4.23	6⅝	6.06	8⅝	7.89
¾	0.69	2¾	2.51	4¾	4.34	6¾	6.17	8¾	8.00
⅞	0.80	2⅞	2.63	4⅞	4.46	6⅞	6.29	8⅞	8.12
1	0.91	3	2.74	5	4.57	7	6.40	9	8.23
1⅛	1.03	3⅛	2.86	5⅛	4.69	7⅛	6.52	9⅛	8.34
1¼	1.14	3¼	2.97	5¼	4.80	7¼	6.63	9¼	8.46
1⅜	1.26	3⅜	3.09	5⅜	4.91	7⅜	6.74	9⅜	8.57
1½	1.37	3½	3.20	5½	5.03	7½	6.86	9½	8.69
1⅝	1.49	3⅝	3.31	5⅝	5.14	7⅝	6.97	9⅝	8.80
1¾	1.60	3¾	3.43	5¾	5.26	7¾	7.09	9¾	8.92
1⅞	1.71	3⅞	3.54	5⅞	5.37	7⅞	7.20	9⅞	9.03
2	1.83	4	3.66	6	5.49	8	7.32	10	9.14

Inches to Millimeters and Centimeters

INCHES	MM	CM	INCHES	CM	INCHES	CM
⅛	3	0.3	9	22.9	30	76.2
¼	6	0.6	10	25.4	31	78.7
⅜	10	1.0	11	27.9	32	81.3
½	13	1.3	12	30.5	33	83.8
⅝	16	1.6	13	33.0	34	86.4
¾	19	1.9	14	35.6	35	88.9
⅞	22	2.2	15	38.1	36	91.4
1	25	2.5	16	40.6	37	94.0
1¼	32	3.2	17	43.2	38	96.5
1½	38	3.8	18	45.7	39	99.1
1¾	44	4.4	19	48.3	40	101.6
2	51	5.1	20	50.8	41	104.1
2½	64	6.4	21	53.3	42	106.7
3	76	7.6	22	55.9	43	109.2
3½	89	8.9	23	58.4	44	111.8
4	102	10.2	24	61.0	45	114.3
4½	114	11.4	25	63.5	46	116.8
5	127	12.7	26	66.0	47	119.4
6	152	15.2	27	68.6	48	121.9
7	178	17.8	28	71.1	49	124.5
8	203	20.3	29	73.7	50	127.0

About the Writers

Sharyn Craig began quilting in 1978 and started sharing her skills by teaching in 1980. She has written seven books, including *Twist 'n Turn, Designing New Traditions, The Wonders of Christmas, Northwind Quilts, Pyramids Plus*, and *Half Log Cabin Quilts*, but she is probably best known as an inspiring teacher who encourages individuality and creativity in her students. Sharyn's "Design Challenge" columns in *Traditional Quiltworks* are full of innovative ideas using traditional formats. She lives in El Cajon, California, with her husband, George.

Jane Hall and **Dixie Haywood** are award-winning quiltmakers who are known for adapting traditional designs using contemporary techniques and innovative approaches. They have co-authored *Perfect Pineapples, Precision Pieced Quilts Using the Foundation Method*, and *Firm Foundations*. Dixie is also the author of the *Contemporary Crazy Quilt Project Book* and *Crazy Quilting with a Difference*, and her articles appear regularly in leading quilt periodicals. Jane is a certified appraiser for old and new quilts. Long-time friends, Jane lives in Raleigh, North Carolina, with her husband, Bob; and Dixie lives in Pensacola, Florida, with *her* husband, Bob. They rely heavily on the telephone, fax, and airlines to function as a team.

Janet Wickell has been quilting for many years, but it became a passion in 1989, when she discovered miniature quilts. She is the sponsor of Minifest, the only national show and seminar devoted to small quilts. For the past several years Janet has been a freelance writer and has contributed to many books for Rodale Press, including eight titles in *The Classic American Quilt Collection* series. She is the author of *Quick Little Quilts*. Janet lives in the mountains of western North Carolina with her husband, daughter, and a growing menagerie of animal friends.

Darra Duffy Williamson is the author of *Sensational Scrap Quilts* and numerous magazine articles on the subject of quiltmaking. In 1989 she was named Quilt Teacher of the Year, and she has traveled extensively, teaching and lecturing at guilds and quilt events. She has served as a technical writer for various Rodale publications. In addition, she is an avid and knowledgeable baseball fan and maintains a notable collection of outrageous socks.

Acknowledgments

We sincerely thank the many people and companies who have generously contributed to this book:

Quiltmakers

Nancy Breland, Morning Glory on page 42

Sharyn Craig, Twist 'n Turn on page 56

Dixie Haywood, Times Three on page 62

Nancy Johnson-Srebro, Pine Tree Delight on page 36

Sue Linker, My Garden (pattern by Country Threads) on page 100, Red and Green Appliqué on page 104, Heartsong on page 68

Little Quilts, Here's to the Bears on pages 68 and 74 from *Little Quilts, All Through the House*; Alphabet Quilt on page 10, from "Greetings" pattern

Suzanne Nelson, Liana's Chicken Salad on page 92, pattern by Country Threads

Sally Schneider, antique Split Nine Patch variation on page 24 (maker unknown), Hawaii Round Robin on page 30, An Apple a Day Is Painless on page 110, Off-Center Log Cabin on page 68

Judy Sogn, September Song on page 68

Judy Sogn and Sue Linker, Whose Quilt Is It Anyway? on page 116

Karen Soltys, Purple Scrap Baskets on page 30

Jill Stolpestad, Basket of Posies on page 20

Darra Duffy Williamson, antique Hovering Hawks (maker unknown) on page 46

Sample Makers

Many of the samples were made by the editor, Sally Schneider. Additional samples were made by Karen Bolesta, Sarah Dunn, Barbara Eikmeier, Nancy Graves, Nancy Johnson-Srebro, Ellen Pahl, Susan Phillips, and Karen Soltys. Thank you to Fabric Expressions for permission to use their pattern "These Guys Don't Melt" on page 66.

Fabrics and Supplies

Bernina of America—sewing machine

Big Board Enterprises—ironing board (1–800–441–6581)

Omnigrid—rotary-cutting mats and rulers

Rowenta—iron

RJR Fashion Fabrics—Thimbleberries fabrics

TRS Designs—Wonderwall Design Wall (1–800–889–1142)

INDEX

Quilting Styles

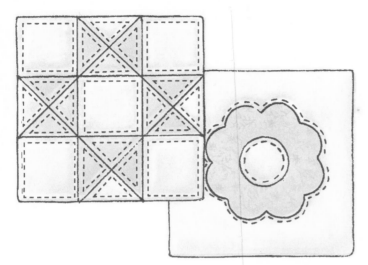

Outline Quilting

Echo Quilting

Single

Double

Crosshatch or Grid Quilting

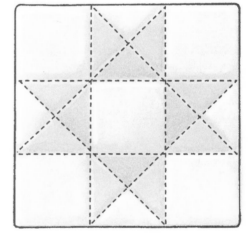

In the Ditch Quilting

Stipple Quilting

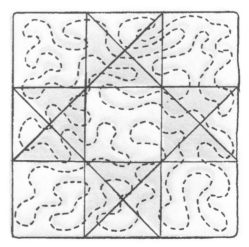

Meander Quilting